Digital SAT Prep: Increase Your Score by 200 Points in 4 Weeks

A Step-by-Step Guide with Targeted Practice, Essential Exercises, and Proven Strategies to Maximize Your Digital SAT Performance

Alex Scorer

DEDICATION

To all the students embarking on this journey of preparation for the Digital SAT: this book is dedicated to you, to your dedication, your determination, and the courage you show as you face challenges to build your future. May you find strength and inspiration in every page, and always remember that your potential is limitless. Believe in your dreams, keep working with passion, and know that the best is yet to come. I wish you all the success you deserve, today and always.

CONTENTS

Introduction: Understanding the Digital SAT Landscape

Overview of the Digital SAT Format and Structure

Welcome to your journey towards mastering the Digital SAT! If you're feeling a mix of excitement and nervousness, know that it's perfectly normal. You're not just preparing for a test; you're investing in your future opportunities. In this introduction, we'll explore what makes the Digital SAT unique, how you can best prepare for it, and why this book will be your trusted companion every step of the way.

The Digital SAT is not just a digital version of the old paper-based test—it's a new experience altogether. The format has been revamped to match the way students today think, learn, and solve problems. The SAT is now fully digital, which means you'll be taking it on a computer or tablet. The overall structure includes two main sections: **Evidence-Based Reading and Writing**, and **Math**. Each section is timed and designed to test your ability to think critically, solve problems, and reason effectively. Knowing the format in advance is like having a roadmap; it can reduce anxiety and boost your confidence because you already know what lies ahead.

Picture this: You sit down at the testing center, and instead of a thick stack of papers, you see a screen with all the tools you need. The questions come one at a time, and you can focus all your energy on just that one without distractions. This new approach is meant to help you engage deeply with each problem, one step at a time.

To help you get familiar with the Digital SAT, let's start with a simple exercise. Take a moment to visualize the test format. Imagine two sections on your screen—Reading and Writing on one side, Math on the other. How do you feel about each section? Write down your thoughts. This exercise can help you identify which areas you might need more support in and set the tone for your study journey.

Why the Digital SAT is Different from the Paper-Based SAT

The digital format changes the way you approach the test, and it's essential to understand these changes to make the most of your study time. One significant difference is how questions are presented and how the test adapts to your performance. The Digital SAT features an **adaptive question format**: the difficulty of questions changes based on how you perform in earlier parts of the section. This means if you answer correctly, you might see harder questions next, which also provide the opportunity for higher scores.

Imagine it this way: You're climbing a hill. At the start, the slope is gentle, but as you continue, it gets steeper. The challenge increases, but so do the rewards. The adaptive nature of the SAT works similarly. If you do well, the test challenges you more—but it also means you're getting closer to the highest scores. To prepare for this, practice with a variety of questions, from easier ones that build your foundation to tougher ones that push your limits.

Don't worry—this is actually an advantage if you prepare well. By practicing a wide range of questions, you can get comfortable with different difficulty levels, increasing your chances of scoring higher. Additionally, no more flipping pages or worrying about where you are on the answer sheet; the digital format streamlines the experience, allowing you to focus solely on the content.

Think of it like a video game: the more levels you complete successfully, the more challenging and rewarding the game becomes. The Digital SAT is your quest, and each level you master means you're becoming a stronger, more confident test-taker.

What to Expect in Terms of Content and Digital Features

The content itself might feel familiar if you've studied for the paper SAT before. You will still encounter passages, data interpretation questions, algebra, and geometry. However, there are some digital features that can make your experience smoother and, if used correctly, can be a powerful tool during the test. For example, the **built-in calculator** for the Math section is a game-changer—no more frantic searching for your calculator. You also have a digital notepad available to jot down ideas or make calculations.

One tip: practice using these tools beforehand. Familiarity is key. You wouldn't want to lose time figuring out how to use a digital calculator while the clock ticks. Instead, get comfortable with these features now, so when test day comes, using them feels second nature. Think of them as your allies.

Let's try a quick exercise: Grab your own calculator and a digital notepad app, and work through a sample math problem from this book. Notice how fast or slow you are, and make adjustments. The more comfortable you are now, the easier it will be to handle these tools under pressure.

The **highlighting tool** is also a great feature for the Reading and Writing sections. You can mark key information directly on the passage, making it easier to keep track of important points. Imagine you're reading a passage on climate change, and you need to remember what the author's main argument is. Use the highlighting tool to mark it, just as you would underline or circle text in a paper test.

Try practicing with an online article—highlight the main ideas and supporting evidence. This will help you train your eye to catch key information quickly, a skill that will be invaluable during the Digital SAT.

The Importance of a Personalized Study Plan for Success

You might be wondering: how do I ensure I'm ready for whatever this test throws at me? The answer lies in a **personalized study plan**. Every student's journey is unique—some of you may excel in Math but need more support with reading comprehension, or vice versa. A personalized study plan helps you focus on your weak areas while maintaining your strengths. It ensures you spend time wisely, without feeling overwhelmed.

Take a moment to reflect on your strengths and weaknesses. Do you find algebra challenging? Are reading passages something you breeze through? Write down your thoughts, and then use this information to build a study schedule that prioritizes areas where you need improvement. This book will guide you through exercises tailored for each type of learner, so you can focus on the sections that matter most to you.

Throughout this book, you'll find suggestions on how to create your own study schedule, tailored to your needs. It's important to assess where you currently stand, set realistic goals, and celebrate small victories along the way. Remember, this is a marathon, not a sprint. Consistency is what will carry you through.

For example, set a goal of completing two math exercises and one reading passage per day. Keep track of your progress in a study journal, and reward yourself when you reach your milestones. These small rewards can help keep you motivated and make the process more enjoyable.

How This Book Will Guide You Step-by-Step to Achieve Your Top Scores

You've taken the first step by picking up this book, and that's a huge accomplishment in itself. This book is structured to **guide you step-by-step** through every topic, strategy, and tip you need. It's designed to be practical and easy to follow, filled with real examples that mirror what you'll face on test day.

For instance, when we dive into the Reading and Writing section, we'll walk through passages together, dissecting them in a way that will make the content easier to understand. You'll learn how to quickly spot key information, understand the author's tone, and tackle tricky questions with confidence. In the Math section, we'll cover every topic from algebra to data analysis, giving you strategies to break down even the most intimidating problems. And there will be practice exercises at the end of each chapter—because the best way to learn is by doing.

Think of this book as a mentor—someone who's been through it all and knows how to help you succeed. You'll receive practical advice, motivational tips, and a clear path forward. We'll celebrate your progress, one chapter at a time. By the end, you won't just be prepared; you'll be ready to excel.

Imagine a student named Alex, who struggled with geometry at first. By following the step-by-step exercises in this book, Alex was able to break down each problem and understand it piece by piece. Alex didn't just memorize formulas—Alex learned how to visualize problems and apply concepts in a practical way. This approach led to a significant improvement in Alex's scores, and it can do the same for you.

So, take a deep breath, know that you are capable, and let's begin this journey together. You have what it takes to conquer the Digital SAT, and I'm here to help you make it happen.

Ready? Let's get started!

Chapter 1: Building a Personalized Study Plan

1.1 Assessing Your Current Skill Level

Creating a personalized study plan is the key to unlocking your full potential on the Digital SAT. To do this effectively, you need to start by understanding exactly where you stand. In this section, we'll walk through how to assess your current skill level and identify your strengths and weaknesses so that you can focus your efforts where they'll have the most impact. Let's get practical, break down each step, and set you on a path to success.

Take an Initial Full-Length Practice Test to Identify Strengths and Weaknesses

The first step in building a successful study plan is to get a clear picture of where you are today. You may be tempted to jump straight into studying specific sections, but before you do that, take a full-length practice test. This isn't just any practice test—it's a benchmark that will give you a realistic sense of how you'd perform if the test were today. Set aside a quiet space and about three hours to take this practice test under real exam conditions. This will give you an honest understanding of your baseline score.

You might ask, "Why do I need to do this now?" Well, think of it like getting a health check-up before starting a workout plan. You need to know your strengths and areas for improvement to build the right strategy. If you don't know where you're starting from, how will you know what to focus on?

Here's a tip: Approach this practice test as if it were the real thing. Set a timer, eliminate distractions, and be honest with yourself. Doing this will help you identify not only content gaps but also the conditions that might affect your performance—like time management or test anxiety.

Analyze Your Scores to Determine Which Areas Need More Attention

Once you've taken the practice test, it's time to dig into your results. This is where the real work begins. Go through each section carefully and identify the areas where you performed well and those where you struggled. Break down your scores by specific sections: **Reading and Writing**, and **Math**.

Start with a broad overview: Did you perform better in Math compared to Reading? Or was it the other way around? Now, drill down deeper. If you struggled with the Math section, which specific topics—like algebra, geometry, or data analysis—were the toughest? If the Reading section gave you trouble, was it understanding the main idea, analyzing tone, or interpreting evidence?

To make this easier, create a checklist. Write down each topic, and next to it, mark whether it's a strength or an area for improvement. For example:

- Algebra: Needs improvement

- Geometry: Strength

- Reading main ideas: Strength

- Analyzing tone: Needs improvement

By being specific, you're creating a clear map of what to focus on. The more detailed your analysis, the more effectively you can prioritize your study sessions.

Set Realistic Goals for Score Improvement Based on Your Target Colleges

Now that you know where you stand, it's time to set some **realistic goals**. Remember, every student's journey is different, and your goals should be specific to your situation. Start by researching the score ranges required by your target colleges. This will give you a sense of what you're aiming for. Let's say your target school's middle 50% SAT score range is between 1300 and

1450. If your initial practice test score was 1100, then you might set a goal to improve by 200-300 points.

Here's where it's important to be realistic. Improvement takes time, and setting goals that are too ambitious can lead to burnout. Instead, break down your overall target into smaller, achievable milestones. For instance, aim to improve by 50 points within the next month. Celebrate each of these small victories, because every step forward brings you closer to your ultimate goal.

To help you stay on track, use a **score tracker**. After each practice test or study session, log your scores and note any patterns you see. Are there certain question types that are consistently giving you trouble? Are there sections where you're making steady progress? This score tracker will be your guide as you refine your study plan.

Exercise: Self-Reflection Checklist

Take a moment to complete the following checklist:

1. Have I taken a full-length practice test?

2. Have I analyzed my scores by section and topic?

3. What are my top three strengths?

4. What are my top three areas for improvement?

5. What is my score goal for the next month?

Motivational Story: How Alex Improved Step-by-Step

To illustrate why assessing your skill level is so important, let's look at Alex's story. Alex was a high school junior who initially found the Math section intimidating. After taking a full-length practice test, Alex realized that while geometry was a strength, algebra was a significant weakness. By focusing on algebra-specific drills and breaking down problems step-by-step, Alex managed to improve steadily. Over the course of three months, Alex's Math score went up by 150 points.

The key was not to try to master everything at once, but to focus on one specific weakness at a time. Alex set small, achievable goals and celebrated each milestone. You can do the same—start with assessing where you are today, and then work consistently towards improvement.

Action Step: Take your first practice test, analyze your results, and write down your strengths and weaknesses. Use these insights to start building your personalized study plan.

By taking this first step, you're already ahead of the game. Let's move forward with confidence, knowing that every bit of effort you put in now will pay off when it matters most. Ready to take that test? Let's get started!

1.2 Creating a Study Schedule that Fits Your Life

Creating a study schedule that works for you is one of the most powerful steps you can take on your journey to conquer the Digital SAT. The key to success is to develop a plan that fits seamlessly into your life, while also pushing you to stay consistent. In this section, we'll break down how to structure your time until test day so that every moment of preparation is effective and manageable.

Break Down Your Available Time Until Test Day into Manageable Chunks

Let's start with the big picture: How much time do you have until your test day? Whether it's three months or six weeks, breaking down your time into manageable chunks will make the entire process less overwhelming. Picture your schedule as a puzzle—each small piece is a study session, and when you put them all together, they form a clear path to your success.

Start by mapping out how many weeks you have left until the test. Then, think about how much time you can realistically dedicate to studying each week. For example, if you have ten weeks until the test, and you can study five days a week for an hour each day, you have a total of 50 study sessions to work with. Don't worry if you have a busy schedule—consistency matters more than the total number of hours. Even just 30 minutes of focused study time can make a significant difference if you stick with it.

Here's a practical exercise: Take out a calendar or planner and mark your test date. Then, decide which days you can commit to studying. Make sure to include some buffer time for unexpected events. Seeing your plan on paper can help make it feel more tangible, which is a big motivator.

Allocate More Time to Areas Where You Scored Lower

Now that you have an idea of how much time you have, let's decide how to use it. Your practice test results from the previous section should be your guide. Allocate more time to the areas where you scored lower, as these are the ones that will benefit most from focused attention. This is a great way to make sure that you are targeting the parts of the test that need the most improvement.

For instance, if your practice test showed that you struggle with algebra but excel in geometry, it makes sense to spend more time each week on algebra. A good rule of thumb is to follow a 70/30 rule: 70% of your study time should be dedicated to your weaker areas, while 30% should be spent reinforcing your strengths. This way, you're improving where it's needed most, but still maintaining the skills that are already strong.

To make this even more concrete, let's say you have four study sessions each week. You could spend three of those sessions focusing on a challenging topic like reading comprehension or algebra, and the remaining one on a strength like data analysis. This balanced approach helps you grow evenly across all sections of the test.

Include Regular Practice Sessions, Review Time, and Rest Days

A successful study schedule isn't just about practice—it's about balance. That means making sure you include regular **practice sessions**, **review time**, and most importantly, **rest days**. Each of these components plays a critical role in effective learning.

Practice sessions are when you'll work on learning new content, drilling practice questions, and applying strategies. These should be frequent and consistent. Review time is when you reflect on what you've learned, revisit challenging problems, and make sure the material really sticks. You might set aside time every weekend to review what you covered during the week.

And don't underestimate the power of rest days. Your brain needs time to absorb information, and rest is a crucial part of that process. Trying to study every single day without breaks can lead to burnout, which is counterproductive. Instead, build in at least one or two rest days each week where you can relax and let your brain recharge.

Example: Designing Your Study Week

Let's say you have four weeks until your Digital SAT. Here's how you could structure a typical week:

- **Monday**: Algebra practice (focused on solving equations)

- **Tuesday**: Reading comprehension (working through a passage and answering questions)

- **Wednesday**: Geometry review (going over key concepts)

- **Thursday**: Rest day (take a break and do something enjoyable)

- **Friday**: Full practice section (simulate test conditions for Math or Reading)

- **Saturday**: Review mistakes from Friday's practice session

- **Sunday**: Rest or light review (flashcards, casual reading)

Notice how there's a mix of new practice, review, and rest. This helps keep your study routine dynamic and prevents burnout. The key here is flexibility—adjust this schedule to fit your life and what works best for you.

Motivational Story: How Maya Balanced Her Busy Life

Take Maya, for example. She was a senior juggling school, a part-time job, and SAT prep. Initially, she felt overwhelmed by the thought of adding study time into her already packed schedule. But by breaking down her available time into small, manageable study sessions, she was able to fit in consistent SAT prep. Maya committed to studying four days a week for 45 minutes each, focusing mainly on her weaker areas—particularly the Reading and Writing sections. She built in rest days where she didn't study at all, giving her time to recharge.

Over time, these small, consistent efforts paid off. Maya saw her scores improve steadily, and she eventually reached the target score she needed for her dream college. The lesson here? Even if you have a busy schedule, fitting in regular, focused study sessions can lead to significant improvements.

Action Step: Create Your Weekly Study Plan

Grab a piece of paper or open up your planner, and write out your weekly study schedule. Answer these questions:

1. How many weeks do I have until my test date?

2. How many days per week can I realistically commit to studying?

3. Which areas need the most attention based on my practice test results?

4. What will my rest days look like?

Remember, consistency is your secret weapon. A well-structured schedule is what transforms good intentions into real progress. Take the time now to plan it out, and you'll thank yourself later.

Ready to Schedule Your Success?

Now that you've learned how to create a study schedule that fits your life, it's time to put it into action. Remember, the best study schedule is the one that works for you—one that you can stick to, that keeps you focused, and that allows you the flexibility to live your life. Let's take that next step towards success, one study session at a time!

1.3 Customizing Your Study Resources

Choosing the right study resources is like building the perfect toolkit—each tool has a specific purpose that will help you overcome the challenges of the Digital SAT. In this section, we'll guide you on how to select and customize the most effective materials for your study plan, so you can maximize your strengths and address your weaknesses without feeling overwhelmed.

Choose Study Materials that Target Your Weaknesses

The first step in customizing your study resources is to choose materials that directly address your unique needs. Not all students are the same, and neither are their study paths. Start by asking yourself: Where do I need the most improvement? Is it algebra, reading comprehension, or perhaps time management? Identifying these areas will help you select the right tools to support your journey.

If algebra is one of your weaker areas, focus on detailed practice problem sets that help you understand and reinforce foundational concepts. Similarly, for reading comprehension, use interactive tools that allow you to practice analyzing passages and finding evidence efficiently. The key is to select resources that directly address where you need improvement.

Our Bonuses to Boost Your Learning: As a bonus, we provide **Advanced Digital SAT Flashcards for Key Concepts**—these flashcards are designed to help you review key terms and strategies efficiently. Flashcards are a perfect way to fit quick practice into your day, especially during short breaks or commutes.

Exercise: Identify Your Weak Areas and Plan Your Resources

Take a few moments to write down the subjects that need the most attention. For each subject, think of one or two study tools you can use. For example:

- Algebra: Advanced Digital SAT Flashcards, targeted practice problems from the book.

- Reading Comprehension: Mini eBook: "Mastering SAT Math in 30 Days", interactive quizzes.

Mix Digital and Traditional Resources for a Well-Rounded Approach

A balanced study routine should involve a mix of digital and traditional study resources. Digital tools, such as video lessons and interactive quizzes, are great for adding variety and can make concepts easier to understand visually. On the other hand, traditional resources like printed practice problems and worksheets are useful for focused, distraction-free study time.

Think of your study approach as preparing for a marathon. Sometimes, you need high-energy bursts, like interactive quizzes to keep things lively, and at other times, you need slow, consistent endurance, like reading and annotating from a printed workbook. By combining both digital and traditional resources, you're giving yourself the versatility to adapt based on how you're feeling and what you need on any given day.

Our **Digital SAT Mind Map Templates** are also excellent tools for visualizing complex concepts and seeing how different ideas are connected, which is incredibly useful when studying topics like reading analysis or math strategies.

Incorporate Exclusive Tools to Enhance Your Preparation

To ensure that you are making the most of your study time, consider incorporating exclusive tools that add value to your preparation. Our **Advanced Digital SAT Flashcards** provide a simple yet powerful way to reinforce key concepts in a structured way, breaking down complex problems into easy-to-understand parts. These flashcards are ideal for revisiting challenging topics and ensuring you remember the most important details.

Example: Creating a Customized Study Toolkit

Let's look at an example. Meet Sarah, a student who felt confident in her reading comprehension skills but struggled significantly with SAT Math, especially algebra and data analysis. To address her math weaknesses, Sarah used a combination of **targeted problem sets from our workbook** and **interactive practice quizzes**. She also used the **Advanced Digital SAT Flashcards** during her daily commute to solidify key concepts.

Sarah found our **Advanced Digital SAT Flashcards** especially helpful for reinforcing challenging algebraic concepts and ensuring she could recall key formulas and strategies when needed. By balancing these resources, she crafted a study routine that fit her needs perfectly—using printed materials for deep focus, digital tools for variety, and flashcards for extra review. Over time, Sarah's consistent use of her customized toolkit led to significant score improvements in her practice tests.

Action Step: Create Your Own Study Toolkit

It's time to create your personalized study toolkit! Take a moment to write down each subject you need to improve in. Next to each subject, list one core resource and one bonus tool you will use. For example:

- **Math**: Targeted practice sets from the book, Advanced Digital SAT Flashcards.

- **Reading & Writing**: Digital SAT Mind Map Templates, Advanced Digital SAT Flashcards.

Remember that the key to a successful study routine is consistency and customization. The more your resources align with your needs and learning style, the more efficient your preparation will be.

Stay Focused and Motivated

Selecting the right resources is about quality, not quantity. By choosing the tools that work best for you, you'll avoid the overwhelm that often comes with an overabundance of options. Instead, you'll have a well-curated toolkit that's tailored to your success. Keep adding small but steady efforts to your routine, and you'll soon see the results you're aiming for.

Ready to build the perfect study toolkit and set yourself up for Digital SAT success? Let's keep moving forward, step by step!

1.4 Tracking and Adjusting Your Progress

Creating a study plan is only the beginning. To make sure that all your efforts truly pay off, you need a way to track your progress and make adjustments along the way. In this section, we'll discuss how to set up a system to monitor your practice test scores, evaluate your progress regularly, and fine-tune your study plan as needed. This approach will help you stay motivated and ensure that every study session brings you closer to your goal.

Set Up a Tracking System (Physical or Digital) to Monitor Your Practice Test Scores

Tracking your progress is key to keeping yourself accountable and staying motivated. It's like watching your fitness results after weeks of workouts—it keeps you going and shows that your hard work is making a difference. You can create a simple tracking system that works best for you, whether it's a physical notebook or a digital spreadsheet.

A **physical notebook** can be a great option if you enjoy the process of writing things down. Use a notebook to record your scores after each practice test, jotting down which sections you improved on and where you need more work. This tactile approach helps reinforce your progress and makes your improvements feel more tangible.

On the other hand, a **digital tracking system**, such as a spreadsheet or a dedicated app, can make it easier to visualize your progress over time. You can use tools like Google Sheets to plot your practice test scores in a graph, giving you a clear picture of how your performance is improving week by week. Plus, digital systems allow you to easily calculate your average scores and identify trends that might not be immediately obvious.

Exercise: Set Up Your Tracking System

Take a moment to decide whether you prefer a physical or digital system. Then, create a simple chart or table where you can record the following details after each practice test:

- **Test Date**

- **Score for Each Section (Math, Reading & Writing)**

- **Areas of Improvement**

- **Next Steps**

By regularly updating your tracking system, you will be able to see the progress you're making, which is incredibly motivating as you move forward.

Evaluate Progress Regularly and Adjust Your Study Plan as Needed

Once you have a tracking system in place, the next step is to evaluate your progress regularly. This means setting aside time, ideally every two weeks, to sit down and review your scores. Ask yourself some critical questions:

- Which sections have shown the most improvement?

- Are there any areas where progress seems to have stalled?

- What specific topics need more focused study?

Regular evaluation helps ensure that you're not just studying, but studying smart. If you find that one section is still lagging behind, consider dedicating more time to that subject in your upcoming study sessions. For example, if your Math scores have improved but your Reading & Writing scores have plateaued, it might be time to allocate extra sessions to practice reading comprehension or grammar.

Example: Adapting Your Plan for Success

Let's look at how regular evaluation worked for Alex, a student preparing for the Digital SAT. Alex noticed that his Math scores were steadily increasing, but his Reading scores weren't improving at the same rate. After looking over his tracking system, he realized that he was spending twice as much time on Math practice compared to Reading. By adjusting his study schedule to give equal focus to Reading, Alex was able to bring his Reading scores up significantly within the next month.

This type of adjustment doesn't just keep your study sessions effective—it also boosts your confidence. When you see an area improve after making a specific change, it reinforces that your efforts are paying off, which motivates you to keep going.

How to Analyze Your Performance After Each Practice Test

Taking a practice test is only valuable if you learn from it. After completing each test, set aside some time to do a thorough analysis. Start by reviewing all of your mistakes, not just noting which questions you got wrong, but understanding **why** you got them wrong. Was it due to a lack of knowledge, a misinterpretation of the question, or simply a careless mistake?

Step-by-Step Analysis Process:

1. **Review Mistakes in Detail:** Write down each question you missed and determine the reason behind your mistake. Categorize errors into groups, such as "concept misunderstanding" or "calculation error."

2. **Identify Patterns:** Look for patterns in your mistakes. Are there certain types of questions that consistently trip you up? This insight is crucial for understanding where you need to focus more attention.

3. **Create an Action Plan:** For each mistake, decide on an action step. For example, if you missed a geometry question because you forgot a key formula, write down a plan to review that formula and practice similar problems. This turns each mistake into a concrete learning opportunity.

Motivational Story: Turning Mistakes into Wins

Consider Maria, who was initially discouraged by her mistakes on practice tests. But by using each mistake as a learning tool, she began to see consistent improvement. Instead of feeling defeated, Maria wrote down every wrong answer and made sure she understood it before moving on. Over time, her scores climbed, and she eventually reached her goal. Remember, mistakes are not setbacks—they are stepping stones to better understanding and higher scores.

Action Step: Analyze Your Last Practice Test

Take your most recent practice test and go through each incorrect answer. Write down the type of mistake and what you will do differently next time. Turn this analysis into a positive experience by focusing on the improvements you can make moving forward.

Stay Motivated by Celebrating Small Wins

Tracking your progress is not only about identifying areas for improvement—it's also about recognizing the small victories along the way. Every improvement, no matter how small, is a step closer to your goal. Did you manage to increase your score by 20 points in Math? Celebrate it! Use these milestones as motivation to keep pushing forward.

Consider rewarding yourself for reaching certain benchmarks. Whether it's taking a break, enjoying a treat, or sharing your progress with someone who supports you, celebrating small wins helps maintain your motivation and makes the journey more enjoyable.

Ready to Track and Conquer?

With a clear tracking system, regular evaluations, and a positive approach to analyzing your practice tests, you have all the tools you need to continuously improve. Remember, this process is about progress, not perfection. Every step you take brings you closer to your Digital SAT goals. Let's keep tracking, adjusting, and succeeding—one step at a time!

1.5 Staying Accountable and Motivated

Building and following a personalized study plan is a significant step toward conquering the Digital SAT, but staying accountable and motivated is what will truly carry you through the journey. In this section, we'll explore how to keep yourself on track by involving others, using tools to stay organized, and ensuring you maintain a healthy and positive mindset throughout your preparation.

Involve a Friend, Family Member, or Tutor to Keep You Accountable

One of the best ways to stay accountable is to involve someone else in your study process. This could be a friend who is also preparing for the SAT, a family member, or even a tutor. When someone else knows your goals, it's much easier to stay committed. You don't want to let them down, and they can also provide encouragement when you need it most.

Consider creating a **weekly check-in routine** with your accountability partner. For instance, you could agree to meet every Sunday to review what you've accomplished and discuss your goals for the upcoming week. This could be done in person, over video chat, or even just by sharing a quick text update. The point is to have someone who can celebrate your wins with you and help you stay on track if you start to fall behind.

Example: Sarah and Her Accountability Partner

Sarah found herself procrastinating on her SAT study plan, so she decided to ask her older brother for help. Each week, they would sit down on Sunday night to review Sarah's practice test scores and talk about what she would work on next. Knowing that her brother would be asking her about her progress kept Sarah motivated, and the supportive conversations helped her see her improvements more clearly. By involving someone else, Sarah was able to stick to her study schedule more consistently and stay motivated throughout the process.

Use Study Apps or Calendars with Reminders to Stay on Track

Sometimes, staying accountable can be as simple as having a good system for managing your time. Study apps or calendars can be incredibly effective tools to help you stay organized and consistent. A well-planned calendar, whether digital or physical, can keep you reminded of your daily study sessions, practice tests, and upcoming goals.

You might use a **digital calendar**, such as Google Calendar, to set reminders for each study session. This way, your phone or computer will prompt you when it's time to study. Alternatively, if you enjoy the satisfaction of crossing off tasks, a **physical planner** can be a great tool to keep track of your progress and visually see how much work you're putting in.

Exercise: Set Up Your Study Reminders

Take a moment now to set up reminders for your study sessions. Whether you're using a digital calendar or a physical planner, schedule at least three study sessions per week, and make sure you get notified when it's time to sit down and focus. Treat these study sessions as appointments with yourself—don't skip them!

How to Avoid Burnout and Maintain Consistent Motivation

Staying motivated is often easier said than done, especially when studying for something as challenging as the Digital SAT. There will be days when you feel like giving up, and that's completely normal. The key is to have strategies in place that help you avoid burnout and maintain a steady pace.

First, **take regular breaks**. Studying for hours without resting is counterproductive. Instead, use techniques like the **Pomodoro method**, which involves studying for 25-minute blocks followed by a 5-minute break. These breaks will keep your mind fresh and prevent exhaustion.

Second, remember to **celebrate small wins**. Did you improve your practice test score by 10 points? That's amazing! Treat yourself to something you enjoy, like a favorite snack or a relaxing walk. These rewards will keep you focused on your progress rather than just the destination.

Story: Avoiding Burnout—Mark's Experience

Mark was initially very enthusiastic about studying for the SAT, but after a few weeks, he found himself feeling overwhelmed and unmotivated. To avoid burnout, Mark decided to change his approach. He started setting smaller, achievable goals and rewarded himself whenever he hit them. If he completed three study sessions in a week, he would treat himself to a movie night. By focusing on manageable goals and building in rewards, Mark was able to maintain his motivation and avoid burnout.

Action Step: Plan Your Rewards

Think of three small rewards that you can give yourself each time you hit a study milestone. Write them down and keep them visible—maybe on your desk or in your study planner. These could be simple, like a favorite dessert, an episode of your favorite show, or a short call with a friend. The important thing is to have something positive to look forward to, which will keep your motivation high.

Stay Consistent with a Positive Mindset

Maintaining a positive mindset is just as important as following your study plan. There will be times when progress feels slow, or when you struggle with certain types of questions. When that happens, remember that every student goes through ups and downs. The key is to keep pushing forward and reminding yourself why you're doing this—whether it's to get into your dream college or to prove to yourself what you're capable of.

Ready to Stay Accountable and Motivated?

Staying motivated and accountable isn't just about studying hard; it's about studying smart, staying consistent, and making sure you enjoy the journey. Find an accountability partner, set up reminders, celebrate your wins, and make sure you're giving yourself the care and support you need along the way. This journey may have its challenges, but you are more than capable of overcoming them—one step at a time!

Chapter 2: Adapting to the Digital SAT Format

2.1 Navigating the Digital SAT Interface

The Digital SAT format is new, and getting comfortable with its interface is crucial to performing well on the test. In this section, we'll guide you through everything you need to know about navigating the digital environment—from using the provided tools to moving efficiently between questions and managing any potential technical issues. By the end of this section, you'll feel much more confident about tackling the test on a computer screen, knowing exactly what to expect.

A Comprehensive Guide to Using the SAT's Digital Tools

The Digital SAT comes equipped with several tools designed to help you during the test, including an **online calculator**, **highlighting features**, and a **note-taking tool**. Understanding how and when to use these tools will make your test-taking experience smoother and more effective.

- **Online Calculator:** During the Math sections that allow a calculator, you will have access to an on-screen digital calculator. It's similar to most standard calculators, but it's embedded within the test interface. Make sure you practice with this calculator during your preparation, as familiarity will save you precious time on test day. For example, if you're comfortable navigating the digital calculator, you won't waste time searching for functions like square root or parentheses.

Tip: Take time during practice to solve some problems using the digital calculator. Set up a few timed drills to help you get used to working efficiently with it.

- **Highlighting Feature**: You can highlight important parts of a question or passage directly on the screen. This feature is especially useful in the Reading and Writing sections. Highlighting helps you stay focused on key information, such as specific details or evidence that might be useful in answering the question. Practicing with this feature during your prep will help you develop a method for staying organized while working through lengthy or complex passages.

Exercise: When practicing reading comprehension, make it a habit to use the highlight feature to underline the main ideas, key terms, or evidence that supports an argument. This will not only help you stay focused but also reduce the amount of re-reading you need to do.

- **Note-Taking Tool**: There's a built-in note-taking feature that allows you to jot down brief notes. This can be incredibly handy if you need to work out a problem in Math or remember key points when analyzing a passage. The note-taking tool acts like a scratchpad—use it to work through tricky questions step by step without losing track of your thoughts.

Example: During a complex algebra problem, you can use the note-taking tool to keep track of intermediate steps. This helps avoid mistakes and provides a clear view of your thought process.

How to Efficiently Move Between Questions and Sections in the Digital Test

Navigating a digital test is different from flipping pages in a booklet. On the Digital SAT, you can move forward and backward between questions within each section. It's important to understand how to use the navigation buttons effectively to keep track of which questions you have answered and which you need to revisit.

The test interface will indicate which questions are **unanswered** or **flagged for review**. If you're unsure about a question, don't spend too much time on it. Instead, flag it and move on—you can always come back later if you have time. This approach ensures you don't get stuck on a difficult problem and miss out on answering questions that you might find easier.

Tip: During practice tests, try simulating the process of flagging questions and moving on. This will help you become comfortable with making strategic decisions under timed conditions.

Tips for Dealing with Technical Issues or Distractions During the Exam

Taking a digital test means there's always a possibility of **technical issues** or unexpected distractions. However, preparing mentally for these situations will help you stay calm if they occur.

- **Stay Calm and Inform the Proctor**: If you experience technical difficulties, such as the screen freezing or issues with the digital calculator, stay calm and raise your hand to inform the test proctor immediately. They are trained to handle these situations and will assist you to ensure you don't lose valuable time.

- **Minimize Distractions**: Make sure you're familiar with the testing environment, whether it's at your school or a test center. Practice focusing on your screen and blocking out other distractions during your study sessions. You could even practice in a slightly noisy environment at times to build resilience to minor disturbances.

- **Practice With Timers and Simulations**: Create mock test environments at home. Set a timer and work through a practice test without pausing. This will help you simulate the time constraints and potential distractions of the actual test day, making you more adaptable and confident.

Motivational Story: Navigating the Digital Format—Jessica's Success

Jessica was initially nervous about taking the SAT in a digital format. She found it difficult to adjust to reading long passages on a screen and using the online calculator. Instead of letting this fear take over, Jessica decided to spend extra time familiarizing herself with every feature of the digital SAT. She practiced using the highlighting and note-taking tools and even set up her practice area to mimic the testing environment. On test day, Jessica felt prepared and comfortable, knowing exactly how to navigate the interface, and ultimately achieved the score she needed to get into her dream college.

Action Step: Get Comfortable with the Interface

Spend at least one practice session each week using the digital tools available for the SAT. Familiarize yourself with highlighting, note-taking, and the on-screen calculator. The more comfortable you are with these features, the more effectively you can use them to your advantage during the actual exam.

Ready to Master the Digital Interface?

The Digital SAT interface is here to help you succeed, but it's essential to know how to use it effectively. By practicing with the digital tools, learning to navigate efficiently between questions, and preparing for any technical hiccups, you'll be well-equipped to tackle the test with confidence. Embrace the digital change, practice regularly, and turn the interface into your ally on test day!

2.2 Familiarizing Yourself with Digital Tools

The Digital SAT format brings a new set of tools to the test-taking experience, and becoming familiar with these digital features can give you a significant advantage. In this section, we'll walk you through the most important tools, from the calculator to highlighting and annotation features, and how to best use online resources to simulate the digital test environment. Remember, the key to success is practice, and soon enough, these tools will feel like second nature to you.

Step-by-Step Instructions on How to Use the Digital SAT's Calculator

The **digital calculator** is a key resource available during certain Math sections of the Digital SAT. Unlike the physical calculators you may be used to, the digital version is embedded directly in the interface. Here's a step-by-step guide to ensure you're comfortable using it:

1. **Access the Calculator**: When you're on a math problem that allows calculator use, you'll see a calculator icon. Clicking on it will bring up the calculator tool. Practice opening and closing it quickly so you can efficiently transition during the test.

2. **Using Common Functions**: The digital calculator includes all the basic functions—addition, subtraction, multiplication, and division— as well as more advanced operations like square roots and exponents. Take time to practice with these functions so that you don't need to search for them on test day.

3. **Avoid Over-Reliance**: Remember, the calculator is a tool—not a crutch. It's there to help with calculations that are cumbersome by hand, but understanding the problem and knowing how to approach it is key. Try solving some practice problems without the calculator first, and use it only when you really need to.

Exercise: Set aside time to solve ten math problems using the digital calculator. Focus on speed and accuracy—becoming familiar with where each function is located will save you precious seconds on test day.

Best Practices for Using Highlighting and Annotation Features Effectively

The **highlighting** and **annotation** features of the Digital SAT are powerful tools to help you stay organized, particularly in the Reading and Writing sections. Here's how you can use them effectively:

- **Highlighting Key Information**: When reading a passage, use the highlight feature to mark key points such as main ideas, supporting details, or important evidence. This helps in quickly locating relevant information when answering questions. It also helps maintain focus and reduces the need to re-read lengthy sections.

Tip: As you read each paragraph, pause briefly to decide if there's a key piece of information you should highlight. Highlight sparingly—only mark the truly important parts to avoid clutter.

- **Annotations for Extra Clarity**: Use the annotation tool to jot down short notes, such as summarizing a paragraph in one line or noting why a particular piece of information is important. For example, if a question asks you about the author's tone, you can annotate the passage with terms like "sarcastic" or "optimistic" when you spot cues that indicate tone.

Example: Imagine you are reading a passage that discusses environmental policies. Highlight the main claim and annotate phrases that indicate the author's perspective, such as "urgent need" or "economic consequences." This will make it easier to reference the passage when answering detailed questions.

Simulating the Digital Test Environment with Online Resources

Practicing in an environment that closely resembles the real test can significantly boost your confidence and reduce anxiety on test day. Here's how you can simulate the digital SAT environment:

1. **Use Official Practice Platforms**: The College Board offers practice tests that emulate the Digital SAT experience. Make it a habit to use these official platforms, as they provide an authentic look and feel of the test interface, including tools like the digital calculator, highlighting, and note-taking.

2. **Practice Timed Sessions**: Set a timer for yourself as you work through practice questions. The goal is to mimic test conditions as closely as possible, which means sticking to the time limits for each section. This will help you get comfortable with the pacing and minimize surprises on test day.

3. **Create a Comfortable Study Space**: Try to create a similar environment to what you'll have on test day. Sit at a desk, use a laptop or desktop computer, and remove any potential distractions. The more familiar you are with the surroundings, the more at ease you'll feel during the actual exam.

Motivational Story: Learning to Trust the Tools—Alex's Journey

Alex initially felt overwhelmed by the digital tools on the SAT. The calculator seemed cumbersome compared to his trusty handheld version, and the highlighting feature felt awkward. Instead of letting this discourage him, Alex dedicated 30 minutes each day to practice using these tools. He would take one reading passage and practice highlighting, or solve a few math problems with the on-screen calculator. Over time, these tools became second nature to him. On the day of the exam, Alex felt confident navigating the interface, and his familiarity with the digital tools helped him save valuable time, ultimately boosting his score.

Action Step: Practice with the Tools Weekly

Dedicate at least one practice session each week to using the digital tools. Spend time working with the digital calculator, highlighting key information, and making brief annotations. The more you practice, the more comfortable you will be, and this familiarity will translate into more efficient test-taking.

Ready to Take On the Digital Tools?

Familiarizing yourself with the Digital SAT tools is all about practice and patience. The more you engage with these features during your preparation, the more natural they will feel on test day. Make these tools your allies—use them effectively, practice consistently, and take charge of the digital format to maximize your performance. You've got this—one tool at a time, you're getting closer to your goal!

2.3 Time Management in the Digital Format

Time management is one of the most critical skills for excelling in the Digital SAT. Unlike the paper-based version, the digital format has unique navigation and tools that require a strategic approach to pacing. In this section, we'll explore how to manage your time effectively, move seamlessly between questions, and maintain your focus during a long exam. Remember, mastering time management is a key factor that can make a significant difference in your scores.

Strategies for Pacing Yourself in a Digital Format

The digital SAT presents a new way of interacting with questions and sections. Instead of flipping through pages, you will be clicking through screens. This means adapting your pacing to the new format is essential.

- **Set Time Benchmarks**: Break down each section into smaller, manageable segments. For instance, if you have 65 minutes for a Reading section with five passages, aim to spend about 12 minutes per passage. Set these mini-goals to keep track of your progress and avoid spending too much time on any single question.

Tip: During practice sessions, use a stopwatch to time how long it takes you to finish each passage or set of questions. This will give you a clear sense of your pacing and help you identify where you need to speed up.

- **Don't Get Stuck—Move On**: It's easy to get hung up on a difficult question, especially when the interface lets you focus on one question at a time. If you find yourself spending too long on a particular problem, flag it, move on, and come back later. Remember, each question carries the same weight, so maximizing the number of attempted questions is crucial.

Exercise: Practice flagging difficult questions and moving forward during mock tests. The more you train yourself to move on, the less likely you are to get bogged down on test day.

- **Use the Navigation Tools Wisely**: The digital SAT interface allows you to easily move between questions within a section. Make use of this feature to revisit questions you've flagged. Having a clear plan for reviewing flagged questions at the end can save time and reduce anxiety.

How to Manage Time When Navigating Between Questions and Using Digital Tools

Time management in the digital environment is all about efficiency. Here are a few strategies to help you manage your time effectively while navigating between questions and using the SAT's digital tools:

- **Highlight Key Information Quickly**: In the Reading and Writing sections, use the highlight feature to mark critical information efficiently. This can help you locate important points faster when answering questions. Practicing this will make the process almost automatic, saving valuable seconds.

Example: When reading a passage, highlight key arguments or shifts in tone. This will help you quickly reference them later when answering related questions.

- **Know When to Use the Calculator**: The on-screen calculator can be a great help during Math sections, but it's also a potential time trap if used inefficiently. Get familiar with when to use it and when to perform quick calculations mentally or by hand. For problems that are straightforward, avoid the calculator altogether to save time.

Tip: Practice doing simple calculations in your head to reduce dependency on the calculator. Use the calculator only when it's absolutely necessary or when dealing with more complex operations.

- **Prioritize Easier Questions First**: Each question carries equal weight, regardless of its difficulty. Start by answering the questions you find easiest, then circle back to the more challenging ones. This strategy helps you secure points early on and builds confidence, especially under timed conditions.

The Importance of Maintaining Focus During a Long Digital Exam

The Digital SAT requires sustained focus over several hours. Here are some strategies to help maintain your concentration throughout the exam:

- **Take Strategic Mental Breaks**: Although you cannot physically leave your seat, you can take small mental breaks between sections or even questions. Close your eyes for a few seconds, take deep breaths, and reset your mind. These brief pauses can help you recharge and stay sharp throughout the exam.

- **Develop a Pre-Test Routine**: Before the actual exam, create a routine that helps you focus. This could involve a short meditation, listening to calming music, or even practicing a few deep-breathing exercises. Developing a consistent pre-test routine can help you enter the test with a calm and focused mindset.

- **Stay Present**: During the exam, it's normal for your mind to drift, especially during long reading passages. When you notice your attention starting to wane, gently bring your focus back to the question at hand. One strategy is to repeat the question or prompt to yourself—this helps you stay grounded and keeps your attention where it needs to be.

Motivational Story: How Proper Pacing Helped Michael Excel

Michael was anxious about managing his time on the Digital SAT. During his practice sessions, he often found himself stuck on difficult questions, which left him with little time for the remaining ones. To overcome this, Michael developed a habit of using the flagging tool. He would spend no more than one minute on each question before deciding whether to answer or flag it. This strategy allowed him to complete all questions within each section, and he used the final minutes to return to flagged questions. On test day, Michael felt in control of his pacing, and this strategy helped him score higher than he had on any of his practice tests.

Action Step: Practice Timed Mini-Tests

Set a timer and practice answering a set of 10 questions within a specific time limit. Focus on moving through the questions efficiently, flagging challenging ones, and returning to them only after completing the rest. This will help you get used to making quick decisions about when to move on, ultimately making your time management stronger.

Are You Ready to Master Time Management?

Time management is the backbone of a successful SAT strategy. By pacing yourself effectively, navigating the digital tools efficiently, and maintaining focus throughout the test, you're setting yourself up for success. Remember, the goal isn't perfection—it's progress. Every time you practice under timed conditions, you're improving your ability to stay calm, focused, and in control. Keep practicing, stay strategic, and trust in your preparation—you've got this!

2.4 Common Pitfalls with Digital Tests and How to Avoid Them

Transitioning to the Digital SAT can be challenging, especially if you're accustomed to traditional paper-based tests. However, by understanding common pitfalls and how to avoid them, you can navigate the digital format more effectively and maximize your performance. In this section, we'll explore some of the most common mistakes students make, how to prevent over-relying on digital tools, and strategies for handling digital fatigue during the exam.

Understanding Common Mistakes When Transitioning to a Digital Format

Switching from a paper-based test to a digital one requires adapting to a new interface and pacing strategy. Let's go over some common mistakes students make when facing this transition:

- **Not Practicing Enough with the Digital Interface**: One of the biggest mistakes is jumping into the Digital SAT without having practiced on a similar digital platform. The interface, navigation buttons, and tools like highlighting and calculators all function differently compared to paper. Failing to practice in a simulated environment can lead to confusion and lost time during the actual test.

Tip: Familiarize yourself with the official practice platforms that simulate the real test environment. Spend time understanding how to navigate between questions, use the digital tools effectively, and review flagged items. Practice makes progress, and every session will help you feel more at ease with the interface.

- **Ignoring the Question Review Feature**: The digital SAT offers a "flag for review" option, which allows you to mark questions that you're unsure about. A common mistake is to either ignore this feature altogether or overuse it. Not flagging questions means you

31

might forget to come back to them, while flagging too many can create unnecessary anxiety toward the end of the test.

Strategy: Be deliberate about flagging—use it when you genuinely need more time on a question but avoid flagging questions if you've given a solid answer. During practice, work on developing a balanced approach that minimizes stress.

Avoiding Over-Reliance on Digital Tools

The digital format of the SAT provides convenient tools like the calculator and highlighting, but relying on these tools too much can actually hinder your performance. Here's how to strike the right balance:

- **The Calculator Trap**: The on-screen calculator can be both a blessing and a curse. While it's helpful for certain calculations, it can also slow you down if you use it excessively. Many simple arithmetic calculations are faster to solve mentally or on paper than they are on the digital calculator.

Tip: Practice solving simpler problems by hand, and only use the calculator for more complex equations. Remember, every second counts, so don't let the calculator be a crutch that slows you down.

Example: Consider a question involving basic multiplication. Instead of spending time clicking on numbers in the on-screen calculator, try doing it mentally. For example, multiplying 7 by 8 is something you should memorize or quickly calculate, as relying on the calculator for such simple tasks can waste valuable time.

- **Overusing Highlighting and Annotations**: Highlighting and annotation features can be extremely helpful, but it's easy to get carried away. Over-highlighting can make passages cluttered and harder to read, while writing too many annotations can take time away from answering questions.

Strategy: Use highlighting sparingly. Focus only on main ideas, crucial evidence, or key words. Practice during your study sessions by highlighting just one or two critical elements per paragraph—this will make it easier to locate important information without overwhelming yourself.

How to Handle Digital Fatigue During a Long Exam Session

Digital tests require staring at a screen for extended periods, which can cause digital fatigue. If not managed properly, fatigue can lead to decreased concentration and errors. Here are practical strategies to help you combat digital fatigue:

- **Take Micro-Breaks**: During the exam, you won't be able to leave your seat, but you can still give your eyes and mind short, refreshing breaks. Every time you complete a question, take a deep breath and blink slowly. This will help reduce the strain on your eyes and briefly reset your focus.

- **Adjust Your Sitting Posture**: Sitting in one position for too long can make you feel fatigued more quickly. Whenever you complete a section, adjust your posture—sit up straight, roll your shoulders back, and stretch your neck slightly. These small movements help improve blood flow and reduce stiffness, keeping you more comfortable and alert throughout the exam.

- **Manage Your Environment**: If you're taking the test at a designated testing center, you might not have full control over your environment. However, you can prepare by practicing in different environments during your prep sessions. Get used to minor distractions, as this will help you maintain focus even if conditions aren't perfect on test day.

Story of Overcoming Digital Challenges—Emma's Experience

Emma was initially overwhelmed by the thought of taking the SAT in a digital format. During her early practice sessions, she found herself overusing the highlighting tool and relying heavily on the calculator for every math problem, which made her feel rushed at the end of each section. Emma decided to change her approach by setting strict rules for herself—she could only highlight one phrase per paragraph, and she would mentally solve all simple calculations. She also practiced micro-breaks and adjusted her posture regularly during long sessions. By the time the actual test arrived, Emma felt much more in control. She finished each section with time to spare and achieved a score higher than she had ever reached in her practice.

Action Step: Practice Smart Tool Usage

During your next practice test, set rules for yourself: limit your use of the calculator to only complex problems and highlight no more than one or two phrases per paragraph. Pay attention to how these rules affect your pacing and clarity. With consistent practice, you'll find yourself more confident and efficient when using digital tools.

Ready to Conquer the Digital Challenges?

Avoiding common pitfalls is about recognizing where things can go wrong and having a plan to address them. By practicing efficiently, balancing your use of digital tools, and managing digital fatigue, you can turn potential obstacles into opportunities for growth. Remember, the Digital SAT might feel different, but with the right strategies, you can use its features to your advantage. Keep practicing, stay aware of your habits, and trust in your preparation—you've got this!

2.5 Practicing with Digital Simulators

Using digital simulators is one of the most powerful ways to prepare for the Digital SAT. By practicing in an environment that mimics the actual test, you become familiar with the tools, the interface, and the pacing required to succeed. In this section, we'll explore why digital simulators are so valuable, recommend some of the best platforms for practice, and show you how to interpret your practice data to continually improve your study strategy.

The Value of Using Digital Simulators for Real Test-Like Practice

The digital SAT format is new for many students, and diving into it without proper preparation can be overwhelming. Digital simulators offer a realistic testing experience that helps you understand the tools, the pacing, and even the mental stamina needed for the actual exam.

- **Build Familiarity with the Interface**: Digital simulators give you a realistic experience of the SAT interface. You can practice using the on-screen calculator, navigating between questions, and making use of the highlighting and annotation features—all without the pressure of the actual exam day. Familiarity can reduce anxiety and improve your confidence.

Example: Imagine the difference between entering a completely new testing environment versus walking into a setting that feels familiar because you've practiced with it many times before. By using a simulator, you can avoid the stress of learning how the system works on the day of your test.

- **Pacing Yourself in Real Time**: One of the biggest challenges of the SAT is managing your time efficiently. Simulators allow you to practice under real test conditions, with timed sections that help you get accustomed to pacing. This helps prevent the common issue of running out of time during certain sections.

Tip: Use the simulator to practice time management techniques like setting benchmarks for each section or flagging questions to revisit later. These drills will help you develop a sense of how quickly you should move through questions to maximize your score.

- **Reduce Test Anxiety**: Familiarity with the format and tools reduces uncertainty, which in turn lowers test anxiety. The more you practice under real conditions, the more you build the mental endurance and calm mindset needed to tackle the actual exam. Remember, practice leads to confidence, and confidence leads to success.

Recommendations for the Best Online Digital SAT Practice Platforms

To get the most out of your preparation, it's crucial to choose high-quality simulators that accurately reflect the actual test environment. Here are some recommended platforms that offer excellent digital SAT simulation experiences:

- **College Board Official Practice**: The College Board offers official digital SAT practice tests that are the best reflection of the actual exam. These tests use the same format, question types, and tools that you will encounter on test day. It's highly recommended to begin with these to get the most accurate experience.

- **Khan Academy**: Khan Academy, in partnership with the College Board, provides free SAT practice tests that closely emulate the official SAT environment. Their platform also provides personalized feedback based on your performance, helping you focus on your weaker areas.

- **Other Online Tools**: There are other online tools that provide practice questions and allow you to simulate the test environment. While not all third-party tools perfectly replicate the SAT interface, many can still offer valuable practice, especially if you want to focus on specific sections or types of questions.

Tip: Make a habit of practicing at least one full-length test on an official platform each month as part of your study plan. This will help you track your progress and make adjustments where needed.

How to Interpret Simulator Data to Improve Your Study Strategy

Practicing with simulators isn't just about answering questions—it's also about learning from your mistakes and adapting your strategy. Here's how to make the most out of your practice data:

- **Track Your Timing**: After completing a practice test, review how long you spent on each section and even on individual questions. If you're consistently running out of time in a particular section, you need to adjust your pacing. Identify if you're spending too much time on harder questions and consider changing your strategy to move on more quickly.

Exercise: After each practice test, make a note of which questions took the longest to answer. Reflect on whether it would have been better to skip and revisit them. Use this information to set specific time goals for each type of question in your next practice test.

- **Analyze Your Mistakes**: Simply getting a question wrong isn't the end—it's a chance to learn. When reviewing incorrect answers, try to determine why you got it wrong. Was it due to a lack of knowledge, a careless mistake, or a misinterpretation of the question? Once you know the reason, you can tailor your study sessions to address these gaps.

Example: Let's say you missed several questions in the Math section because you misread what the problem was asking. In your next study session, you could practice taking extra care to read each question twice before attempting to solve it. This adjustment could make a big difference in your future performance.

- **Use Performance Metrics to Guide Future Study**: Most digital simulators provide detailed performance metrics, showing your strengths and weaknesses across different question types. Use these metrics to guide where you spend your study time. Focus on the areas where you scored lowest and allocate more practice sessions to those topics.

Tip: Set a goal for each study session based on your simulator results. For example, if you struggled with data analysis questions, dedicate one or two study sessions that week specifically to practicing data analysis problems.

Story of Growth—How Simulators Helped Daniel Improve

Daniel was nervous about taking the SAT in a digital format because he was used to working with paper tests. In his first digital practice test, he found the on-screen calculator awkward and struggled with pacing. Instead of getting discouraged, Daniel made a plan. He practiced weekly using a digital simulator and focused on his weak areas—particularly using the digital tools effectively and adjusting his pacing. Over time, Daniel saw noticeable improvements. By the time his actual test date arrived, Daniel felt at ease with the interface, and his score improved significantly compared to his initial practice tests. The practice with digital simulators helped Daniel turn uncertainty into confidence.

Action Step: Plan Your Simulator Practice Routine

Schedule at least one full-length digital practice test every two weeks. After each test, spend time analyzing your results: note the sections where you struggled, track your time, and plan future study sessions based on these findings. The key is not just to practice but to practice thoughtfully, using the insights from your simulator results to continually improve.

Are You Ready to Take Advantage of Digital Simulators?

Digital simulators are a powerful tool that can bridge the gap between preparation and test day success. By practicing in a realistic setting, understanding the strengths and weaknesses revealed in your data, and adjusting your study strategy accordingly, you're setting yourself up for real improvement. Keep practicing, stay positive, and remember—every session is another step toward achieving your top score!

Chapter 3: Mastering the Math Section of the Digital SAT

3.1 Understanding the Structure of the Math Section

The Math section of the Digital SAT is often one of the most challenging parts of the test for many students, but with a clear understanding of its structure and some effective strategies, it becomes much more manageable. In this section, we'll break down the components of the Math section, explore the types of questions you'll encounter, and dive into the key math concepts you need to master.

Breakdown of Calculator and Non-Calculator Sections

The Math section of the Digital SAT is divided into two distinct parts: **calculator** and **non-calculator**. Understanding the differences between these sections and knowing how to approach each one strategically is crucial for maximizing your score.

- **Calculator Section**: In this part, you're allowed to use a calculator, either an on-screen version or your own approved device. This section typically contains problems that involve more complex calculations, and having a calculator helps you solve them more efficiently. However, the key is not to become overly reliant on the calculator—many questions can still be solved faster through estimation or mental math.

Tip: Practice using your calculator effectively during your preparation. For instance, be familiar with basic functions and how to quickly input values. Time is limited, so knowing how to navigate your calculator will save you seconds that add up.

- **Non-Calculator Section**: This part is designed to test your ability to perform calculations without technological aid. It often includes questions where mental math or quick paper-and-pencil calculations are needed. The key to doing well here is practice—getting comfortable with doing calculations by hand, especially under timed conditions, can make a big difference.

Example: You might encounter a question like, "What is 17% of 200?" This is something that can be calculated quickly in your head or with a bit of practice on paper. Mastering these skills helps prevent you from getting bogged down when a calculator isn't available.

Here's a practical method to solve it: First, convert 17% to a decimal by dividing by 100, which gives 0.17. Then, multiply 0.17 by 200. The result is 34. This method can be done mentally or with quick paper calculations. Mastering these skills helps prevent you from getting bogged down when a calculator isn't available.

- **Types of Questions: Multiple Choice and Grid-Ins**

The Math section includes two main types of questions: **multiple choice** and **grid-ins**.

- **Multiple Choice**: Most of the Math questions are multiple choice, with four answer options. The key here is to solve the problem efficiently and then double-check if your answer matches any of the given choices. An effective strategy for multiple choice is **plugging in values**—when the algebra gets complex, sometimes testing values in the answer choices is the fastest way to find the right solution.

Tip: When practicing, challenge yourself to solve the problem first and then find ways to double-check your answer by substituting values from the choices. This will help build confidence in your approach.

- **Grid-In Questions**: These are also known as **student-produced responses**, where you fill in the answer on your own rather than selecting from choices. This type tests not only your math skills but also your accuracy since there's no opportunity to guess from provided answers.

Best Practice: Always **double-check your calculations** when working with grid-in questions. Since there are no options to choose from, simple errors can lead to missing the question entirely. Practicing grid-in questions with a timer helps improve both accuracy and speed.

Key Math Concepts Tested in the SAT

The SAT Math section focuses on a range of core mathematical concepts. Here's a breakdown of the most important ones to master:

- **Algebra**: The backbone of the SAT Math section. You'll see questions that require solving linear equations, systems of equations, and understanding functions. Focus on getting comfortable with manipulating algebraic expressions and balancing equations.

Example: You might encounter a problem like "$2x + 3 = 11$." Practicing how to isolate x quickly will be essential for answering these types of questions efficiently.

- **Geometry and Trigonometry**: This includes questions on angles, triangles, circles, and basic trigonometric relationships. Remember that most geometry questions will use familiar formulas like area, circumference, and the Pythagorean theorem. Flashcards can be a great way to memorize these key formulas.

Tip: Keep a list of essential geometry formulas handy and review them regularly. Practicing with a few sample problems each day will ensure these formulas are always fresh in your mind.

- **Statistics and Probability**: These questions assess your understanding of data interpretation, mean, median, mode, and probability. These problems often involve interpreting charts or graphs and extracting information to solve a problem. The key here is to carefully analyze the data presented and apply your knowledge logically.

Exercise: After each practice test, review any statistics problems you got wrong. Ask yourself whether you misunderstood the chart, missed key data, or incorrectly applied a statistical concept. With consistent review, you'll find these problems much less intimidating.

Story of Growth—How Understanding Math Structure Helped Mia

Mia found herself intimidated by the Math section of the Digital SAT because she struggled to finish within the time limits. She often found herself spending too much time on questions that required the calculator, which left her rushed in the non-calculator part. Mia decided to change her approach by breaking down her preparation: she dedicated separate study sessions to mastering the non-calculator skills and made it a point to only use her calculator when necessary. She also practiced grid-in questions until she felt comfortable filling in the answer boxes without second-guessing herself. By test day, Mia had transformed her anxiety into confidence and saw a significant improvement in her overall score.

Challenge for You: Test Your Understanding

To put these strategies into practice, try this exercise:

1. Take a practice set of ten Math questions, with a mix of calculator and non-calculator problems.

2. Time yourself—set a goal to complete each question within two minutes.

3. Identify which questions took you the longest and why. Did you struggle more with non-calculator questions? Were the grid-ins harder to complete? Write down your reflections and adjust your next study session accordingly.

Key Points to Remember

- Familiarize yourself with both calculator and non-calculator sections. Learn when to use the calculator to save time but also practice mental math for speed.

- Multiple choice questions can sometimes be solved faster by plugging in values. For grid-ins, accuracy is key—double-check your calculations.

- Focus on mastering algebra, geometry, and statistics, as these are core areas tested in the Math section.

By understanding the structure of the Math section, you're already on your way to feeling more confident. Each type of question has its own strategy, and by practicing consistently and thoughtfully, you can turn this often daunting section into an opportunity to show your strengths. Keep going—step by step, you're getting closer to mastering the Math section!

3.2 Reviewing High-Yield Math Topics

Mastering the Math section of the Digital SAT requires a strong grasp of specific, high-yield math topics that are most likely to appear on the test. In this section, we will cover the key concepts, including algebra, geometry, trigonometry, and data analysis, which are crucial for maximizing your SAT score.

Focus on Algebra: Solving Equations, Inequalities, and Functions

Algebra forms the backbone of the SAT Math section, and it's vital to be comfortable solving a variety of algebraic problems. Topics include solving equations, inequalities, and working with functions.

- **Solving Equations**: Be prepared to solve both linear and quadratic equations. Practice isolating variables and factoring expressions. Remember, efficiency matters—always look for ways to simplify calculations before solving.

Challenge for You: Try to solve these equations to put into practice what you have just learned:

1. Solve $3x - 7 = 11$

2. Find x for the equation $x^2 - 4x - 5 = 0$

Check your answers by comparing them with the step-by-step solution available at the end of the chapter.

Example: Consider the equation "$2x + 5 = 15$". To solve for x, subtract 5 from both sides to get "$2x = 10$", and then divide by 2 to find "$x = 5$". The goal is to make sure each step brings you closer to isolating the variable.

- **Advanced Tip**: For quadratic equations, practice factoring and using the quadratic formula. For example, if you have "$x^2 - 5x + 6 = 0$", try factoring it into "$(x - 2)(x - 3) = 0$", which gives solutions $x = 2$ and $x = 3$. Familiarity with factoring can save you significant time on the test.

- **Common Mistake to Avoid**: Always double-check your signs when moving terms across the equals sign. A small mistake in sign can lead to incorrect answers.

- **Inequalities**: These are similar to equations, but with greater-than or less-than symbols. Practice manipulating inequalities, and remember that if you multiply or divide by a negative number, you need to flip the inequality sign.

Challenge for You: Solve these inequalities and graph the solution:

1. $-2x + 3 > 7$

2. $4 < 3x - 5 \leq 13$

Try to represent the solutions on a number line to better visualize them.

Tip: Practice graphing inequalities on a number line. This helps you visualize solutions, especially when dealing with systems of inequalities.

- **Advanced Exercise**: Solve compound inequalities, such as "$-3 < 2x - 5 < 7$". Start by isolating "x" in the middle by adding 5 to all parts of the inequality, giving "$2 < 2x < 12$". Then divide everything by 2 to find "$1 < x < 6$".

- **Common Pitfall**: When dealing with inequalities involving multiplication or division by negative numbers, remember to reverse the inequality sign. For example, if "$-2x > 8$", dividing by "-2" gives "$x < -4$".

- **Functions**: You will need to understand how to interpret and manipulate functions, including evaluating functions for specific inputs and analyzing their behavior.

Challenge for You: Consider the function $f(x) = 2x^2 - 3x + 4$. Find $f(2)$ and $f(-1)$. Then, try to identify if the function has a minimum or maximum using the graph.

Compare your answers with the solution guide available at the end of the chapter.

Confronta le tue risposte con la guida di soluzione disponibile alla fine del capitolo.

Exercise: Take a few practice problems where you need to substitute values into functions. For example, if $f(x) = 3x + 2$, find $f(4)$. Start by replacing x with 4: $f(4) = 3(4) + 2 = 14$.

- **Interpreting Function Graphs**: Practice reading graphs of functions and identifying key features like intercepts, maxima, and minima. For instance, if you are given the graph of f(x), determine where it crosses the x-axis and y-axis.

- **Transformations of Functions**: Be familiar with basic transformations, such as shifts and stretches. For example, if $f(x) = x^2$, then $g(x) = (x - 2)^2$ represents a shift of the parabola 2 units to the right.

- **Challenge**: Given a function $h(x) = 2x + 3$, determine $h(x + 1)$. Substitute "x + 1" in place of "x", giving $h(x + 1) = 2(x + 1) + 3 = 2x + 2 + 3 = 2x + 5$.

Review of Geometry and Trigonometry Basics and Their Applications

Geometry and trigonometry questions often test your understanding of shapes, angles, and their properties. It's important to review key formulas and know when to apply them.

- **Geometry Basics**: Be sure to memorize essential geometry formulas, such as those for calculating the area and perimeter of common shapes (triangles, circles, rectangles). Understanding relationships between angles, especially in triangles and circles, is key.

Challenge for You: Find the area and circumference of a circle with a radius of 5 cm. Then, calculate the area of a triangle with a base of 10 cm and a height of 8 cm.

These problems will help you better memorize key geometry formulas.

Example: If you're given a right triangle with legs of 3 and 4, use the Pythagorean theorem to find the hypotenuse: $a^2 + b^2 = c^2$, which gives you $3^2 + 4^2 = c^2$, or $9 + 16 = 25$. So, $c = 5$.

- **Advanced Applications**: Practice finding missing angles in different types of triangles, including isosceles and equilateral. For example, if you have an isosceles triangle with base angles of 50°, you can determine the third angle by subtracting the sum of the base angles from 180°, which gives 80°.

- **Coordinate Geometry**: Be comfortable working with points on the Cartesian plane. For instance, know how to calculate the distance between two points using the distance formula: $d = \sqrt{(x2 - x1)^2 + (y2 - y1)^2}$. Practice applying this formula to find distances and midpoints.

- **Circles**: Understand the properties of circles, including calculating the circumference (C = 2πr) and area (A = πr²). Additionally, know how to work with sectors and arc lengths, as these may appear in more advanced problems.

- **Trigonometry**: Basic trigonometry, like sine, cosine, and tangent, might appear. Practice using SOH-CAH-TOA to solve for missing sides or angles in right triangles.

Challenge for You: In a right triangle, angle A is 30°, and the side opposite this angle is 5 cm long. Find the length of the hypotenuse using the sine ratio.

Check your answer by comparing it with the step-by-step method described in the following section.

Verifica la tua risposta confrontandola con il metodo passo-passo descritto nella sezione successiva.

Tip: Keep a quick-reference sheet of trigonometric ratios and practice applying them to different triangle problems. For example, if you know the opposite side and hypotenuse, you can use sine to determine the angle.

- **Using the Unit Circle**: Though not always required, understanding the unit circle can help with trigonometry questions. The unit circle allows you to easily determine the sine and cosine of common angles (like 30°, 45°, and 60°).

- **Special Right Triangles**: Memorize the properties of 30-60-90 and 45-45-90 triangles. For instance, in a 30-60-90 triangle, the sides are in a ratio of 1:√3:2. Knowing these properties allows you to quickly solve for missing side lengths.

- **Inverse Trigonometric Functions**: Be prepared to use inverse trigonometric functions to find angles when given side lengths. For example, if you know the opposite side and adjacent side, use arctan (or $\tan^{-1}$) to find the angle.

Understanding Data Analysis, Statistics, and Interpreting Graphs

Data analysis is another crucial part of the SAT Math section. These questions often require you to interpret information presented in charts, tables, or graphs.

- **Statistics Basics**: Key topics include mean, median, mode, and range. Understanding these concepts is essential for answering data interpretation questions.

Challenge for You: Consider the following data set: {4, 8, 8, 15, 20}. Calculate the mean, median, mode, and range. Compare your answers with those provided in the solutions section.

These exercises will help consolidate your understanding of basic statistics.

Example: If you have the data set {3, 7, 7, 10, 15}, the mean is calculated by summing the values (3 + 7 + 7 + 10 + 15 = 42) and dividing by the number of values, which is 5. Thus, the mean is 8.4.

- **Median and Mode**: The median is the middle value when the data set is arranged in order, and the mode is the value that appears most frequently. For the data set {3, 7, 7, 10, 15}, the median is 7, and the mode is also 7.

- **Range**: The range is found by subtracting the smallest value from the largest value. For this data set, the range is 15 - 3 = 12. Understanding how to quickly determine these values is essential for success.

- **Advanced Concepts**: Be familiar with standard deviation and variance, as they occasionally appear in more challenging data analysis questions. Standard deviation measures how spread out the values in a data set are, while variance is the square of the standard deviation.

- **Interpreting Graphs**: You might be asked to extract information from bar graphs, line graphs, or scatter plots. Practice reading these visuals quickly and accurately to identify trends, values, or relationships.

Challenge for You: Look at the following bar chart showing the sales of four products (A, B, C, D) in one month. Answer the questions:

1. Which product recorded the highest sales?

2. What is the difference between the sales of products B and D?

This challenge will help you improve your ability to interpret graphs quickly.

Exercise: Look at a sample graph and try to answer questions about it within a time limit. This helps build your speed and accuracy in interpreting data.

- **Trends and Relationships**: Be sure to practice identifying positive, negative, or no correlation in scatter plots. Understanding the direction and strength of a relationship between variables can help answer questions more effectively.

- **Bar Graphs and Line Graphs**: For bar graphs, be precise in comparing heights to determine quantities. For line graphs, practice finding the rate of change by looking at the slope of the line between two points.

- **Pie Charts**: Occasionally, you may need to interpret pie charts. Practice determining the percentage of the whole represented by different sections, and use basic fraction-to-percent conversions to answer related questions.

Challenge for You: Test Your Understanding

Practice interpreting a sample graph with different types of questions. Here's one to try:

1. Look at a given line graph representing the growth of a plant over 12 weeks.

2. Determine in which week the plant showed the highest growth rate.

3. Describe any patterns or anomalies you notice.

This will help reinforce your skills in interpreting data presented visually and understanding trends effectively.

3.3 Time-Saving Strategies for Math

When it comes to the Math section of the Digital SAT, knowing how to solve problems is important—but knowing how to solve them *efficiently* is what can set you apart. This section will provide practical strategies to help you save time, keep focused, and make smart decisions about which questions to tackle first. By mastering these strategies, you will gain confidence in your ability to manage time effectively, ensuring you have the chance to answer every question you can.

How to Quickly Identify Which Questions to Skip or Solve First

One of the biggest mistakes students make is trying to solve every question in the order presented. Not all questions are created equal—some are quick wins, while others are more complex and time-consuming. Here are some guidelines to help you decide:

- **Scan the Section First**: Quickly glance through the questions at the beginning. Identify the questions that seem straightforward. These might be simple algebraic equations or basic geometry problems that you can solve in under a minute.

- **Mark and Skip Difficult Questions**: If you find a question that looks challenging or involves complex calculations, mark it and move on. The Digital SAT allows you to easily return to skipped questions later. Don't let a single difficult problem consume too much time and disrupt your flow.

- **Use the "Two-Minute Rule"**: If a question takes more than two minutes and you're still struggling, it's a signal to skip it for now. Come back to it if time permits at the end.

Example: If you come across a question that involves multiple steps, such as a complicated system of equations, it may be better to skip it initially and return once you've completed the simpler problems. The goal is to gather as many points as possible, and prioritizing easier questions helps maximize your score.

Challenge for You: Look through a set of practice math problems. Spend only 30 seconds per question to determine if it's a "quick win" or if it requires more effort. Practice categorizing them as either "solve now" or "skip and return."

Using Shortcuts for Solving Algebraic Equations Efficiently

Algebraic equations can often be simplified using shortcuts. Recognizing opportunities to simplify before diving into calculations can save precious time.

- **Combining Like Terms**: If you see an equation like "$3x + 4 - 2x = 7$," combine similar terms first. This will make the equation easier and faster to solve: then solve .

- **Plugging In Simple Values**: For equations where variables are present, try substituting easy numbers (like 1 or 0) to simplify the process and quickly find potential answers.

- **Using Reverse Operations**: Instead of doing a lengthy calculation, think about working backward from the answer choices. Plug the answer choices into the equation to see which one works.

Example: Suppose you have the equation . Add 7 to both sides to get , and then divide by 2 to get . By thinking in steps, you can avoid unnecessary operations and solve equations more efficiently.

Challenge for You: Solve the following equation using a shortcut: . Can you find a quicker way to isolate "x"? Check your answer against the solution provided at the end of the chapter.

Grid-In Question Strategies and Avoiding Common Mistakes

Grid-in questions require you to provide your answer rather than choosing from multiple choices, which can make them more intimidating. However, by following these strategies, you can maximize accuracy and avoid pitfalls:

- **Estimate First**: Before you solve, take a moment to estimate the answer. This helps catch errors before they happen. If you estimate that a value should be around 20 but calculate something wildly different, it's a sign you may have made an error.

- **Be Mindful of Fractions and Decimals**: Grid-in questions sometimes require answers in fractional form. If the answer is a repeating decimal, be sure to round appropriately or use a fraction to prevent errors.

- **Double-Check Units**: Make sure your answer matches the required units. If a question asks for a length in centimeters, but your calculation yields meters, make the necessary conversion.

- **Practice with Precision**: Use practice problems to get comfortable with gridding answers accurately. Make sure to write numbers clearly and align them correctly in the grid to avoid mistakes.

Example: You need to solve for the area of a rectangle with a length of 5.5 and a width of 3. You can use the formula, which gives. Be careful when gridding this answer—make sure it fits correctly, and if decimals are involved, place them accurately.

Challenge for You: Solve the following grid-in question: What is the value of "x" if 2x+3=112x + 3 = 112x+3=11? After finding the answer, practice gridding it to make sure you are comfortable with the process.

Challenge for You: Practice Your Precision: Try solving the following grid-in questions and practice filling in the answer grids:

1. What is the value of "y" if y2=49y^2 = 49y2=49?

2. Find the length of a side if the perimeter of a square is 36 units.

Make sure to practice placing your answers correctly in the grid to avoid losing points due to simple formatting errors.

Key Points to Remember

- **Prioritize Easier Questions**: Solve questions that are simple first and return to the challenging ones later.

- **Use Algebra Shortcuts**: Simplify as much as possible before solving, and plug in numbers to make equations more manageable.

- **Estimate in Grid-Ins**: Estimating answers before solving helps catch errors and gives you a mental checkpoint.

Challenge for You: Apply What You've Learned

Try using the strategies from this section on a real SAT practice set. Set a timer for 20 minutes and practice deciding which questions to tackle first, using shortcuts to solve equations, and completing grid-ins. This will help you build confidence in these time-saving methods and refine your approach.

Success Story: How One Student Improved Their Timing

Anna, a student preparing for the Digital SAT, initially struggled with completing the Math section in time. She found herself getting stuck on difficult questions and running out of time before reaching the end. After learning to prioritize easier questions and using algebra shortcuts, she noticed a significant improvement. During her practice tests, Anna skipped the lengthy questions and completed all the straightforward ones first. This allowed her to return to the harder questions with more focus and less pressure, ultimately boosting her score by 80 points. Anna's story is a testament to how powerful time management can be—sometimes, small changes in strategy make the biggest difference.

Takeaway: Don't let difficult questions hold you back. Focus on what you can solve quickly, and always have a plan to come back to more challenging problems. Efficient use of your time is just as important as knowing how to solve the problems.

3.4 Practice Exercises for Math Mastery

Practice makes perfect, and when it comes to mastering the Math section of the Digital SAT, targeted and consistent practice is key. In this section, we will explore how to identify your weak points and turn them into strengths, incorporate realistic practice tests, and work through detailed examples to improve your overall performance. Remember, every exercise is a stepping stone toward improvement. Let's break down how to use practice effectively and build confidence step by step.

How to Incorporate Targeted Practice for Math Weaknesses

It's important to approach math practice with a strategic mindset. Instead of practicing randomly, focus on the areas that need the most improvement. Here's how to effectively incorporate targeted practice:

- **Identify Your Weak Areas**: Start by reviewing your previous tests or quizzes. Highlight the types of problems you struggled with the most. Whether it's algebraic equations, geometry, or statistics, be honest about where you need more work. This is your opportunity to grow.

- **Create a Schedule**: Dedicate specific time slots each week to focus on these weak areas. It could be 30 minutes every day on geometry if that is your weakest point, or an hour on weekends for mixed problem sets. Consistency will be key in solidifying your skills.

- **Use Mixed Practice Sets**: Once you've identified a weakness and practiced it in isolation, mix in problems from different areas. This simulates the experience of the test, where you'll face a variety of topics back to back. Mixed practice also helps keep your mind flexible and sharp.

Challenge for You: Identify your three biggest math weaknesses. For the next week, spend 20 minutes each day focusing on one of these areas. Make sure to track your progress to see how much more confident you become.

Using Practice Tests to Simulate Test-Day Pressure

Simulating the actual testing environment can be incredibly beneficial when preparing for the SAT. Here's how to make your practice tests as effective as possible:

- **Recreate Test Conditions**: Take practice tests in a quiet room, free from distractions. Set a timer to match the time limits of the actual SAT Math sections. Use only the tools you will have available on test day, such as a calculator (where allowed) and scrap paper.

- **Time Management Practice**: Practicing under time pressure helps you learn to pace yourself effectively. During these tests, note which questions you find yourself spending too much time on. Mark these for review later to determine why they took longer.

- **Analyze Results Thoroughly**: Once you've finished a practice test, don't just look at the score. Dive into each incorrect answer to understand your mistakes. Did you miscalculate? Misinterpret the question? By understanding your errors, you can prevent them in the future.

Challenge for You: Set up a simulated test this weekend. Find a quiet spot, set a timer, and complete a full-length Math section. When you finish, review each answer—even the correct ones—to see if you could have solved them more efficiently.

Detailed Walkthroughs of Practice Questions with Step-by-Step Explanations

Understanding how to approach and solve each type of problem is fundamental to improving your math skills. Let's walk through a few common types of questions you might encounter in the SAT Math section, step by step.

- **Example 1: Solving Algebraic Equations**

  - *Problem*: Solve for x in the equation $3x+5=20$.

  - *Step 1*: Subtract 5 from both sides to get .

    - *Explanation*: Subtracting the constant from both sides helps to begin isolating the variable . This is the first step in reversing the operations applied to .

  - *Step 2*: Divide both sides by 3 to get .

- *Explanation*: Dividing by 3 on both sides ensures that is completely isolated. This step allows us to solve for directly, completing the solution.

  ○ *Final Check*: Plug back into the original equation to verify: , which is true. This confirms our solution is correct.

- **Example 2: Finding the Area of a Circle**

  ○ *Problem*: What is the area of a circle with a radius of 7?

  ○ *Step 1*: Use the formula for the area of a circle, ($A = \pi r^2$).

  ○ *Step 2*: Substitute 7 for r, giving $A = \pi(7)^2$.

  ○ *Step 3*: Calculate . If an approximation is needed, use , which gives .

  ○ *Explanation*: Remember to keep units consistent, and always use the formula accurately. Practicing these types of problems will help you feel comfortable with key formulas.

- **Example 3: Solving a System of Linear Equations**

  ○ *Problem*: Solve the system: x + y = 10 and x - y = 4.

  ○ *Step 1*: Add the two equations to eliminate . This gives .

  ○ *Step 2*: Divide by 2 to get .

  ○ *Step 3*: Substitute back into to find .

  ○ *Explanation*: Systems of equations can often be solved more efficiently by combining or substituting. Practice makes these techniques intuitive.

Challenge for You: Try solving a system of equations similar to the example above. Use different numbers and see if you can solve it step by step without looking at the solution.

Challenge for You: Put Your Skills to the Test Set a timer for 10 minutes and solve the following:

1. Find the value of if .

2. Calculate the area of a rectangle with a length of 8 and a width of 5.

3. Solve the system: and .

Key Points to Remember

- **Target Your Weaknesses**: Spend time on the topics you find most challenging. Improvement happens fastest when you address your gaps.

- **Simulate Real Test Conditions**: Practice tests should feel as much like the real test as possible. This helps you get comfortable with timing and pressure.

- **Break Down Problems Step by Step**: Don't rush through practice problems. Understand each step thoroughly to prevent mistakes on test day.

Success Story: Overcoming Math Anxiety

Mark was initially overwhelmed by the Math section. He found that the timer made him nervous, and he often skipped practice out of frustration. However, by incorporating daily 15-minute practice sessions that focused on his weakest topics, Mark gradually built confidence. He also simulated real test conditions every weekend, which helped him become comfortable under time pressure. Over time, Mark's scores improved significantly—he went from scoring in the 500s to the 700s. His consistent practice and focus on weaknesses made all the difference.

Takeaway: Small, consistent steps lead to big changes. Identify your weaknesses, practice diligently, and simulate the real test environment. You've got this—every step you take brings you closer to your goal.

3.5 Handling Test Anxiety in Math

The Math section of the Digital SAT is one of the most feared parts of the test, and it's completely normal to feel anxious about it. Test anxiety can hold you back from reaching your full potential, but the good news is that it can be managed with the right strategies. In this section, we will explore techniques to manage anxiety specifically during the math section, how to remain calm when faced with difficult math problems, and how to build confidence by mastering the commonly missed questions. Let's face this challenge together—you've got this!

Techniques for Managing Anxiety During the Math Section

It's not uncommon for students to feel a surge of anxiety when they see math problems that seem unfamiliar or difficult. The key is to have strategies to keep that anxiety from taking over. Here are some practical techniques to help you manage anxiety during the test:

- **Breathing Exercises**: One of the simplest ways to calm your mind during a stressful situation is to focus on your breathing. Try the 4-7-8 method: breathe in for 4 seconds, hold for 7 seconds, and exhale slowly for 8 seconds. Doing this a few times can help lower your heart rate and bring a sense of calmness, allowing you to focus better.

- **Positive Self-Talk**: Anxiety often stems from negative thoughts like "I can't do this" or "I'm terrible at math." Replace these thoughts with positive affirmations such as "I am prepared for this" or "I can solve this one step at a time." Reminding yourself that it's okay to make mistakes can also ease some of the pressure.

- **Focus on One Question at a Time**: The sight of many problems can feel overwhelming. Instead of looking at the entire test, remind yourself to tackle one question at a time. Break the test down into smaller, manageable parts—all you need to focus on is the question right in front of you.

Story of Success: Maria, a student who struggled with severe test anxiety, found that practicing mindfulness for 10 minutes every day made a huge difference. Before each practice session, she would take a moment to breathe deeply and visualize herself solving problems successfully. By the time test day arrived, she felt much calmer and improved her math score significantly.

How to Remain Calm When Faced with Difficult Math Problems

Even the best-prepared students face math problems that stump them at first glance. Here are some strategies to keep your cool in such situations:

- **Skip and Return**: If you come across a question that you don't immediately know how to solve, skip it and move on. Mark it, and return to it later if time allows. This approach helps you save valuable time and prevents frustration from building up. Remember, skipping isn't giving up—it's a strategy.

- **Break Down the Problem**: Sometimes anxiety arises because the problem looks complex. Try breaking it into smaller, more manageable parts. Can you identify what the question is asking? Is there a familiar formula that might apply? By breaking it down step by step, the problem can become less daunting.

- **Practice Under Timed Conditions**: Repeated exposure to test-like pressure helps desensitize you to the feeling of anxiety. Practice solving math problems under timed conditions regularly, so you become accustomed to managing your time effectively without panicking.

Challenge for You: The next time you face a difficult problem during practice, consciously apply the "Skip and Return" strategy. See how much time it saves and how it impacts your mindset throughout the test.

Building Confidence by Mastering Commonly Missed Math Questions

Confidence is a powerful tool against anxiety. One of the best ways to build confidence is to work specifically on the types of questions that you commonly miss. Here's how you can do it:

- **Identify Patterns in Mistakes**: Review your past practice tests and identify the types of questions that give you the most trouble. Is it word problems? Geometry? Statistics? Pinpointing these areas allows you to focus your practice on exactly what you need.

- **Targeted Practice**: Once you know your weak spots, spend extra time working through similar problems. If word problems are difficult for you, dedicate some practice sessions entirely to word problems. Over time, you'll find that these questions become easier and less intimidating.

- **Celebrate Small Wins**: Each time you solve a problem that used to stump you, take a moment to recognize your progress. These small victories add up and make a big difference in how you approach the test overall.

Success Story: John used to struggle with trigonometry questions, often missing them during practice. Instead of avoiding them, he decided to dedicate 15 minutes a day to practice just trigonometry. After a few weeks, he noticed he was getting more confident, and eventually, those questions became some of his strongest. The confidence he gained helped him reduce his overall test anxiety.

Key Points to Remember

- **Breathe, Stay Positive, and Focus**: Anxiety is natural, but it doesn't have to control you. Use breathing techniques, positive self-talk, and focus on one problem at a time to manage it.

- **Skip and Return**: Don't let difficult questions derail your focus. Skip and return to them if needed, ensuring you maximize your time effectively.

- **Practice and Celebrate Progress**: Building confidence through practice is one of the most effective ways to manage anxiety. Celebrate every improvement, no matter how small.

Challenge for You: Putting Strategies into Practice

Next time you practice math, take note of the moments when you start feeling anxious. Use one of the anxiety-reducing strategies discussed—like the 4-7-8 breathing method or positive self-talk—and observe how it impacts your ability to solve the problems. Write down your reflections and note any improvements in your mindset.

Key Points to Remember

- **Anxiety is Common**: It's okay to feel anxious—you're not alone.

- **Strategies Work**: Techniques like breathing, positive self-talk, and strategic skipping can greatly reduce your anxiety.

- **Confidence Comes with Practice**: The more you familiarize yourself with challenging problems, the more confident you will become.

You can conquer this test—remember, it's about progress, not perfection. With these strategies, you'll be ready to face any math question with a calmer, more focused mindset. Keep practicing, stay positive, and know that you have the tools to succeed.

SAT Math Practice Questions - Chapter 3-Based Test

Section 3.1: Understanding the Structure of the Math Section

Calculator and Non-Calculator Sections

1. **Calculator Section**: Calculate $(12.5 \times 3.6) + (7.2^2 - 3.4)$

   - A) 98.56

   - B) 100.12

   - C) 93.68

   - D) 95.30

2. **Non-Calculator Section**: What is 19% of 400?
   - A) 60
   - B) 76
   - C) 80
   - D) 94

3. **Mental Math**: If 5x=95, what is x?
   - A) 15
   - B) 17
   - C) 19
   - D) 21

4. **Grid-In**: Calculate the value of $\dfrac{3x+5}{2}$ =20. Solve for x.

5. **Grid-In Practice**: You have a rectangle with an area of 56 square units and one side of 8 units. Find the length of the other side.

Section 3.2: Reviewing High-Yield Math Topics

Algebra, Geometry, Trigonometry, Data Analysis

1. **Algebra (Multiple Choice)**: Solve for x in 4x+3=19.
   - A) 3
   - B) 4
   - C) 5
   - D) 6

2. **Inequalities**: Solve the inequality 3x−5<13.

- A) x<6x
- B) x<7x
- C) x≤6x
- D) x≥7x

3. **Geometry**: A triangle has angles of 45°, 45°, and 90°. If one leg is 6 cm, what is the length of the hypotenuse?
- A) 6 cm
- B) $6\sqrt{2}$ cm
- C) $6\sqrt{3}$ cm
- D) 12 cm

4. **Trigonometry**: If sin A=0.5 and angle A is in a right triangle, what is the measure of angle A?
- A) 30°
- B) 45°
- C) 60°
- D) 90°

5. **Data Analysis**: The following data set represents the number of books read by 5 students in a year: {4, 8, 6, 5, 7}. What is the median?
- A) 5
- B) 6
- C) 7
- D) 8

Section 3.3: Time-Saving Strategies for Math

1. **Quick Wins**: Identify which of these questions you would solve first:

   - A) Solve 4x+7=3.
   - B) Find the area of a circle with radius 5.
   - C) Solve a system of equations with 3 unknowns.
   - D) Integrate a function with respect to x.

2. **Using Shortcuts**: For the equation $7(x-2) = 35$, solve for x.
- A) 5
- B) 7
- C) 9
- D) 11

3. **Reverse Operations**: Given that $y+4=18$, find the value of y.
- A) 12
- B) 13
- C) 14
- D) 15

4. **Grid-In**: Find the value of x if $5x-3=17$.
5. **Precision Practice**: Solve for the area of a square with a side length of 9 units. Grid in your answer.

Section 3.4: Practice Exercises for Math Mastery

1. **Targeted Weakness Practice**: Solve the inequality $-3<2x-5<7$. What is the solution for x?

   - A) $-1< x <6$
   - B) $1< x <7$
   - C) $2< x <8$
   - D) $-2< x <4$

2. **Algebra (Multiple Choice)**: Solve the quadratic equation $x^2-5x+6=0$.
- A) x=2,3
- B) x=1,5
- C) x=-2,3
- D) x=3,5

3. **Geometry (Grid-In)**: A circle has a circumference of 31.4 cm. What is the radius?

4. **Trigonometry**: Given a right triangle where angle A is 60° and the adjacent side is 4 cm, find the hypotenuse.
- A) $4\sqrt{3}$
- B) 8
- C) 5
- D) 6

5. **Graph Interpretation**: A line graph shows the distance traveled by a car over 5 hours. If the car traveled 300 miles in 5 hours, what was the average speed in miles per hour?
- A) 50
- B) 55
- C) 60
- D) 65

Section 3.5: Handling Test Anxiety in Math

1. **Anxiety Management Practice**: If a math problem takes more than two minutes, what strategy should you use?

   o A) Guess and move on

   o B) Skip and return later

   o C) Spend as much time as needed

   o D) Ask for help

2. **Breathing Techniques**: When you feel overwhelmed, what is the suggested breathing method?

   o A) 4-7-8 method

   o B) 2-5-10 method

   o C) 5-5-5 method

   o D) 3-6-9 method

3. **Skip and Return**: Which question type is best to skip initially and return to later?

   o A) Basic arithmetic

o   B) Long word problems

o   C) Simple algebra

o   D) Estimation problems

4. **Practice Under Pressure**: During practice, you realize you missed a question due to a miscalculation. What should you do?

    o   A) Ignore it

    o   B) Understand where you went wrong

    o   C) Guess better next time

    o   D) Spend less time on such questions

5. **Targeting Weakness**: If you commonly miss geometry questions, what is the best practice?

    o   A) Avoid geometry questions

    o   B) Practice them daily

    o   C) Only focus on strengths

    o   D) Skip them on the test

Chapter 4: Excelling in the Reading Section of the Digital SAT

4.1 Understanding the Structure of the Reading Section

The Reading section of the Digital SAT may appear challenging at first, but by understanding its structure and the different types of questions you'll encounter, you can approach it with confidence. In this subsection, I'll guide you through the various types of passages and questions you'll face, providing practical tools to handle each aspect effectively.

Types of Reading Passages

In the Digital SAT, the reading passages fall into three main genres: **literature**, **history**, and **science**. Each genre requires a slightly different approach since the content and style vary. Here's what to expect:

1. Literature Passages: Understanding Characters and Themes

What They Are: Literature passages are usually drawn from novels, short stories, or classic fiction works. They explore universal human themes like relationships, personal challenges, and growth. This genre emphasizes storytelling elements, such as character emotions, motivations, and interpersonal dynamics, which can involve subtle nuances that require close attention.

Characteristics:

- **Tone**: Often descriptive, reflective, or emotional.

- **Focus**: Character development, internal conflict, or relationships between characters.

- **Structure**: These passages often follow a narrative arc with exposition, rising action, and sometimes a climax or resolution.

How to Approach Literature Passages:

1. **Read Actively for Emotional Cues**: Notice words or phrases that reveal character emotions, like "reluctantly" or "joyfully." Emotional cues provide insight into relationships and motivations.

2. **Identify Character Dynamics**: Literature passages often focus on relationships, so pay attention to how characters interact. For instance, is there tension or harmony between them? Are there power dynamics at play?

3. **Focus on Theme and Conflict**: Identify the main theme and any conflict presented, as these are key to understanding the passage's deeper meaning.

Example: Suppose you read an excerpt where two siblings are discussing their future. One is ambitious and eager to leave home, while the other is reluctant and fearful. The dialogue between them might reveal contrasting values and could suggest a broader theme of independence versus security.

Practical Tip: After reading a literature passage, ask yourself questions like:

- o "What are the characters' primary concerns or goals?"

- o "How does each character view the situation differently?"

- o "What theme or lesson might the author be conveying?"

By focusing on these aspects, you'll be better prepared to answer questions on character motivations, themes, and the author's purpose.

---

2. History Passages: Analyzing Arguments and Perspectives

What They Are: History passages often include excerpts from speeches, foundational documents, or analyses of historical events. These passages deal with political, social, or economic issues and usually adopt a more formal tone. They may present an author's perspective on a specific issue or reflect on historical ideals, such as freedom, justice, or equality.

Characteristics:

- **Tone**: Formal, often persuasive or expository.

- **Focus**: Arguments, author perspectives, or ideals related to social, political, or economic themes.

- **Structure**: History passages are often structured around a central argument or viewpoint, with supporting evidence provided throughout.

How to Approach History Passages:

1. **Identify the Author's Thesis Early On**: History passages usually start by introducing a central argument or thesis. Try to pinpoint this thesis quickly, as it provides the framework for understanding the rest of the passage.

2. **Pay Attention to Supporting Evidence**: Authors of history passages often include examples, analogies, or historical references to strengthen their argument. Recognize these as they help clarify the author's position.

3. **Note Any Persuasive Language**: Look for words that convey the author's stance, such as "unjust," "essential," or "inevitable." These terms give insight into the author's attitude toward the topic.

Example: Imagine a passage from a Martin Luther King Jr. speech that discusses justice and equality. The passage's thesis might emphasize the importance of nonviolent protest to achieve social change. Supporting evidence could include references to other successful nonviolent movements or calls to moral principles.

Practical Tip: After reading, ask yourself questions like:

- "What main argument is the author making?"

- "What evidence does the author use to support this argument?"

- "What historical or moral perspective is presented here?"

These steps will help you tackle questions that ask about the author's argument, evidence, and overall message.

3. Science Passages: Grasping Explanations and Findings

What They Are: Science passages draw from topics in biology, chemistry, physics, environmental science, or psychology. They often introduce a concept or present findings from a study or experiment. These passages are more factual and technical, requiring you to understand the main points, results, and implications without getting bogged down in scientific jargon.

Characteristics:

- **Tone**: Objective, descriptive, or analytical.

- **Focus**: Explanations of scientific phenomena, experimental results, or implications of scientific discoveries.

- **Structure**: Science passages typically begin with a hypothesis or introduction to a concept, followed by details of an experiment or findings, and conclude with interpretations or implications.

How to Approach Science Passages:

1. **Identify the Main Idea Quickly**: Science passages often start with the main idea or research focus, followed by details. Understanding this focus helps you organize the rest of the information presented.

2. **Pay Attention to Results and Implications**: Results are often directly related to the questions you'll answer, so note any conclusions, numbers, or comparisons made in the passage.

3. **Don't Get Lost in Technical Details**: While technical terms might be introduced, questions usually focus on the main argument, purpose, or interpretation. Use context clues if you're unfamiliar with specific scientific terminology.

Example: A science passage may discuss a study on renewable energy sources. The main focus might be on solar versus wind energy, with findings suggesting one is more efficient under certain conditions. Implications might include potential environmental benefits or economic impacts.

Practical Tip: As you read, focus on questions like:

- "What is the main point or hypothesis?"

- "What are the key findings or results?"

o   "What conclusions or implications do these results suggest?"

This focus will prepare you for questions about scientific reasoning, key findings, and the broader implications of the study or concept discussed.

Additional Tips for All Passage Types

1. **Time Management**: Each passage has an ideal amount of time you should spend on it, so allocate time wisely. Generally, allow a few minutes to read actively, making mental notes or quick annotations, and save the remaining time for answering questions.

2. **Use Process of Elimination**: Many questions have distractor answers designed to look plausible. By eliminating answers that don't align with the passage's details, you can narrow down your choices.

3. **Practice with Purpose**: For each passage type, try practicing with sample passages in each genre. Look for patterns in how questions are asked, and practice the strategies outlined here to become comfortable with each type.

By understanding the unique characteristics and strategies for each passage type, you'll be equipped to navigate the Reading section with confidence and accuracy.

Types of Questions: Inference, Vocabulary, and Function

Understanding the types of questions you'll face is crucial to mastering the Reading section. These questions are designed to test various skills, including inference, vocabulary understanding, and identifying the function of specific parts of the text. Here's a breakdown:

1. Inference Questions: Reading Between the Lines

What They Are: Inference questions require you to go beyond the explicit information in the text and make logical deductions about what the author or character is implying. These questions test your ability to understand nuances in the text, such as implied attitudes, underlying emotions, or unstated conclusions.

Common Phrases:

*   "The passage suggests…"

- "The author implies…"

- "Based on the passage, it can be inferred that…"

Example Question: *Passage Excerpt*: "Mary stood at the edge of the cliff, watching the waves crash against the rocks below. She pulled her coat tightly around her as the wind howled, yet she couldn't bring herself to turn back."

Question: "What can be inferred about Mary's feelings in this moment?"

Detailed Approach:

1. **Identify Clues**: Notice specific words or phrases that hint at Mary's emotional state—"watching the waves crash," "pulled her coat tightly," and "couldn't bring herself to turn back."

2. **Analyze Word Choices and Imagery**: The imagery suggests an intense, perhaps turbulent inner state, mirroring the stormy environment.

3. **Consider Broader Context**: Based on this, we might infer that Mary feels conflicted or hesitant about a decision or situation in her life, as indicated by her reluctance to leave despite the harsh conditions.

Practice Tip: For inference questions, practice asking yourself what the scene or description *might mean beyond the literal words.* Note shifts in tone or unusual word choices that suggest an underlying message. Try reading a few sentences and writing down what feelings, opinions, or implications you think the author is suggesting without stating directly.

---

2. Vocabulary in Context Questions: Deciphering Word Meaning from Surrounding Clues

What They Are: These questions require you to determine the meaning of a specific word as it's used in the passage. SAT vocabulary questions are not just about knowing definitions; they test your ability to understand how a word functions within its unique context, which can sometimes give the word a specialized meaning.

Common Phrases:

- "In line X, the word 'Y' most likely means…"

- "The author's use of the word 'Z' suggests…"

Example Question: *Passage Excerpt*: "After receiving the news, Jonathan felt a keen sense of urgency, pushing him to act without delay."

Question: "In this sentence, the word 'keen' most nearly means…"

- (A) enthusiastic

- (B) painful

- (C) sharp

- (D) intense urgency

Detailed Approach:

1. **Return to the Sentence Context**: In this sentence, "keen" is describing Jonathan's "sense of urgency," which suggests a heightened, almost pressing need to act.

2. **Use the Process of Elimination**: Options like "enthusiastic" don't fit here, as it doesn't capture the idea of urgency. "Intense urgency" (D) is the best fit since it matches the implied meaning of a pressing need.

3. **Look for Surrounding Clues**: Other words in the sentence, such as "without delay," emphasize the urgency of the situation, helping clarify the meaning of "keen" in this context.

Practice Tip: As you read, underline or circle words whose meanings might not be immediately clear. Try to guess the meaning of the word from context before consulting any outside definitions. This practice builds your skill in determining meaning based on context clues, which is exactly what you'll need in the SAT.

---

3. Function Questions: Analyzing Purpose and Structure

What They Are: Function questions ask about the role a particular sentence, paragraph, or phrase plays within the broader context of the passage. These questions test your understanding of the text's structure and how specific details contribute to the author's argument or purpose.

Common Phrases:

- "What is the function of [specific paragraph/sentence] in the passage?"

- "Why does the author include [specific detail]?"

- "How does [sentence/paragraph] contribute to the author's argument?"

Example Question: *Passage Excerpt*: "In the early stages of his career, Thompson struggled with financial instability. He often worked late hours and took on multiple jobs to make ends meet. This phase of hardship shaped his character and made him resilient."

Question: "What is the function of the second sentence in the author's argument?"

Detailed Approach:

1. **Identify the Main Argument**: Here, the main argument is that Thompson's struggles in his early career built resilience.

2. **Analyze the Role of the Sentence**: The second sentence ("He often worked late hours…") gives specific examples that support the author's argument. It provides concrete evidence of Thompson's hard work, reinforcing the idea that his challenges contributed to his resilience.

3. **Consider Alternative Options**: If asked to choose from options, eliminate those that don't match the sentence's purpose in supporting or elaborating on the main argument.

Practice Tip: Function questions require you to understand both the passage's big picture and the smaller pieces within it. Try summarizing each paragraph or major sentence as you read to clarify how each part contributes to the overall message. This habit will make it easier to answer questions about specific sentence roles during the test.

Interactive Practice Section: Challenge Yourself with Function and Inference

Sample Passage:
"Rebecca's journey from a small, quiet village to the bustling city was not without its challenges. The pace of life in the city initially overwhelmed her, as she found herself surrounded by a constant stream of unfamiliar faces and sounds. However, over time, Rebecca adapted and began to thrive, using the energy of the city as fuel for her creativity."

Practice Questions:

1. **Inference Question**: What can be inferred about Rebecca's initial reaction to the city?

2. **Function Question**: What is the function of the first sentence in setting up the author's portrayal of Rebecca's transformation?

Take a moment to think through each question, and remember:

- For inference, look for hints in word choices like "overwhelmed" and "found herself surrounded," which suggest her initial discomfort.

- For function, recognize that the first sentence sets up the contrast between Rebecca's quiet village life and her later transformation in the city.

4.2 Developing Active Reading Strategies

Active reading is more than just skimming a passage; it's about engaging with the text to retain information, quickly locate key points, and interpret the author's intent. In this subsection, you'll learn the techniques of annotation, identifying main ideas, tone, and purpose, and breaking down complex sentences—each designed to make you an efficient, analytical reader. Let's go through these strategies in depth, with examples and practice prompts to help you put them into action.

Annotating Passages to Quickly Locate Key Information: A Detailed Guide

Effective annotation is like building a mental map of the passage, allowing you to pinpoint essential information, clarify complex ideas, and engage actively with the text. Here, we'll expand on how to make each type of annotation more purposeful and introduce additional techniques to enhance your understanding and retention of the passage content.

Why Annotation Matters

Annotation is more than marking up a passage—it's an active reading strategy that forces you to pause and process information. This processing is crucial on the SAT, where you need to extract and recall key information efficiently. Good annotation helps you:

- **Quickly refer back** to important parts of the passage when answering questions.

- **Organize information visually**, which improves recall and understanding.

- **Engage with the text**, making it easier to identify themes, relationships, and structures.

Advanced Steps for Effective Annotation

Let's delve deeper into each annotation technique, exploring how to apply it in different contexts and how it helps you answer specific question types on the SAT.

1. **Underline or Highlight Main Ideas and Core Statements**

Underlining main ideas is the first step to structuring your understanding of the passage's purpose and message. However, underlining becomes most effective when done selectively, with attention to the author's intent and structural cues.

- o **Focus on Key Sentences**: The main idea often appears at the beginning or end of a passage, especially in non-fiction texts. Look for statements that summarize, emphasize, or clarify the author's main argument.

- o **Identify Supporting Evidence**: In passages with multiple supporting points (common in science and history), underline the core evidence or examples that back up the main argument. This helps you quickly find information if questions ask for supporting details.

Practice Tip: Avoid underlining full sentences if possible. Instead, highlight only the essential parts of a sentence, such as the main idea or a critical fact, as this prevents clutter and keeps your focus on high-impact content.

2. **Circle Key Terms, Names, and Concepts**

This step is especially valuable in passages where specific terms, names, or technical details play a prominent role. Circling these elements helps you:

- o **Track Important Details**: Circle dates, terms, or names that the author revisits, especially if they are central to the passage's argument or narrative.

- o **Identify Repeated Ideas**: If a term appears frequently (such as "urbanization" or "freedom"), this repetition signals its importance. Circling such terms helps you follow recurring themes that may come up in questions.

Example Application: In a passage about environmental conservation, circle terms like "biodiversity," "ecosystem," or "habitat" to help connect specific ideas to the broader environmental theme.

3. **Use Symbols to Mark Patterns, Contrasts, and Areas for Review**

This method is where annotation becomes truly interactive, allowing you to create a visual code that reflects your interpretation of the text. Different symbols prompt you to look back or notice recurring themes, helping you structure your understanding more deeply.

- o **Stars (★) for Themes or Recurring Ideas**: Placing a star by a phrase or sentence can help you track ideas that are central to the author's message. This is especially useful in literature passages, where thematic elements like "identity" or "conflict" are core to the passage.

- o **Arrows (→) for Cause and Effect**: Arrows can be helpful in science passages, where processes and sequences often follow a cause-and-effect pattern. Arrows also work well for tracking arguments that evolve across the passage or for highlighting shifts in perspective.

- o **Question Marks (?) for Areas Needing Further Analysis**: A question mark next to a complex or ambiguous phrase serves as a reminder to revisit that part of the passage. This is particularly useful for unfamiliar vocabulary or scientific explanations, where rereading might clarify meaning in context.

Practical Tip: Make a quick key in the margin with your chosen symbols. Having a reference for your symbols helps you stay consistent in your annotations, ensuring you can understand your markings when reviewing.

Detailed Example of Annotated Passage

Let's apply these techniques to a more detailed example to see how they enhance comprehension. Here's a passage with a few complex ideas that require active reading:

"The rapid spread of digital technology has revolutionized communication across the globe. However, while some argue that this increased connectivity fosters cultural exchange and understanding, others warn that it may lead to the erosion of local identities and traditions. As global platforms standardize content, individual voices can often be drowned out, creating a homogeneous digital culture that overrides local uniqueness."

Annotations:

- **Underline**: "The rapid spread of digital technology has revolutionized communication" (main idea of the first sentence).

- **Circle**: "cultural exchange," "understanding," "erosion of local identities," "homogeneous digital culture" (key concepts that the passage contrasts).

- **Star**: "fosters cultural exchange and understanding" and "overrides local uniqueness" (indicate key themes: positive vs. negative effects).

- **Arrow**: From "increased connectivity" to "fosters cultural exchange" and "drowned out" to "homogeneous digital culture" (to show cause and effect relationships in the passage's argument).

These annotations would help you:

- Quickly locate the main points if questions ask about the overall message of the passage.

- Understand the contrast between positive and negative effects of digital technology on culture, useful for inference questions.

- See the cause-and-effect pattern that the author uses to explain how digital platforms might influence cultural uniqueness.

Practical Exercise: Test Your Annotation Skills

Let's practice with a passage. Try reading and annotating this text, applying the techniques we discussed:

"For centuries, societies have debated the nature of justice, from Plato's philosophical dialogues to modern legal theories. At the heart of these debates lies the question of fairness: Should justice aim to punish wrongdoing or to rehabilitate those who commit offenses? While punitive justice seeks retribution, rehabilitative justice focuses on personal improvement, offering offenders a path to reintegration into society."

Guided Annotation:

1. **Underline** the main idea in the first sentence.

2. **Circle** key terms like "punitive justice" and "rehabilitative justice."

3. **Star** phrases that highlight contrasting views on justice.

4. **Place a question mark** by any part that feels unclear or requires further thought.

Reflect: After annotating, reflect on how this process has helped you understand the passage more deeply. Does it feel easier to answer questions about the author's stance or the main ideas?

Refining Your Annotation Skills

Like any skill, effective annotation improves with practice. As you read more passages, try refining your approach by adjusting your symbols, focusing on different types of details (themes, evidence, etc.), or experimenting with different ways to mark up texts. Over time, your annotations will become more intuitive, allowing you to read actively and engage deeply with any passage you encounter on the SAT.

Identifying the Main Idea, Author's Tone, and Purpose

1. Main Idea: Understanding the Core Message

The main idea of a passage is its central argument or insight, the point the author wants you to remember. It's essential to locate the main idea quickly, as this sets up your understanding of the passage's structure and can guide your approach to related questions.

Advanced Techniques for Finding the Main Idea

- **Identify Topic Sentences in Paragraphs**: In SAT passages, each paragraph often begins with a topic sentence that connects to the central argument. Read these topic sentences closely, as they build on or reinforce the main point.

- **Scan for Repetition and Synonyms**: Authors often reinforce the main idea by repeating certain words or using synonyms that circle back to their core argument. For instance, a passage on conservation may repeat terms like "preserve," "safeguard," and "protect."

- **Distinguish Main Ideas from Supporting Details**: Supporting details, examples, and anecdotes often elaborate on the main idea. These details usually answer "how" or "why" questions, while the main idea answers "what." Ask yourself, "What is the author arguing or describing overall?"

Practice Application

Sample Passage: "The global rise of renewable energy is a testament to technological innovation and environmental awareness. While many countries are committed to reducing their carbon footprints, challenges like cost, infrastructure, and political resistance continue to hinder progress. Nevertheless, renewable energy remains a critical component of a sustainable future."

Steps:

1. **Identify Core Sentences**: The first and last sentences seem central, discussing both renewable energy's importance and the challenges it faces.

2. **Find Repetition**: Notice "renewable energy" and "sustainable future" repeated, indicating a focus on long-term environmental benefits.

3. **Distill the Main Idea**: From these cues, the main idea could be summarized as "The global shift to renewable energy, despite challenges, is vital for a sustainable future."

2. Author's Tone: Revealing Attitude and Perspective

Tone is the author's attitude toward the subject, ranging from supportive and enthusiastic to skeptical or neutral. The tone colors the interpretation of ideas, shaping the reader's perception of the content. Knowing the tone helps interpret the author's stance and the emotional context of the passage.

Advanced Techniques for Determining Tone

- **Examine Descriptive Language**: Look at adjectives and adverbs for emotional or judgmental language. Positive tones use words like "remarkable," "hopeful," or "beneficial," while negative tones might use "concerning," "flawed," or "ineffective."

- **Analyze Verb Choices**: Verbs reveal action and intensity. For instance, "supports" or "promotes" can convey a supportive tone, while "criticizes" or "questions" signal skepticism.

- **Check for Rhetorical Devices**: SAT authors often use rhetorical questions, metaphors, or comparisons to highlight tone. For example, an author might use irony to express doubt or use an optimistic metaphor to signal enthusiasm.

Practice Application

Sample Passage: "Although many believe in the simplicity of healthy eating, the array of processed options suggests otherwise. Supermarkets are filled with packaged products claiming health benefits, yet often these are misleading. Without better regulations, consumers remain at the mercy of food manufacturers' marketing."

Steps:

1. **Look for Emotionally Loaded Words**: Words like "misleading," "mercy," and "marketing" carry negative connotations, suggesting a critical tone.

2. **Identify Rhetorical Devices**: The phrase "consumers remain at the mercy" personifies the food industry as having undue power, hinting at the author's disapproval.

3. **Determine Tone**: The tone here can be described as critical or disapproving, as the author questions the integrity of food marketing.

3. Purpose: Uncovering the Author's Goal

The purpose reflects *why* the author wrote the passage. Understanding purpose clarifies the intent behind the author's choice of details, structure, and tone. SAT passages commonly aim to inform, persuade, entertain, or explain, and discerning the purpose reveals the framework of the text.

Advanced Techniques for Identifying Purpose

- **Consider the Type of Evidence Presented**: Informational texts often include data, statistics, or expert opinions. Persuasive texts, on the other hand, may emphasize emotional appeals, personal anecdotes, or calls to action.

- **Look for Calls to Action or Recommendations**: Persuasive passages often end with a suggestion or conclusion aimed at influencing the reader's viewpoint. If the author proposes a specific action or change, this likely indicates a persuasive purpose.

- **Assess Structural Elements**: The structure of the passage often aligns with its purpose. For example, passages that methodically build an argument or cite sources aim to persuade or inform, while those that use vivid imagery and storytelling aim to entertain or evoke emotion.

Practice Application

Sample Passage: *"With climate patterns growing increasingly unpredictable, cities around the world are investing in resilient infrastructure. Projects range from flood barriers in coastal cities to drought-resistant crops in rural areas. By adapting to these challenges, communities hope to mitigate the impacts of climate change."*

Steps:

1. **Analyze Evidence and Details**: The passage provides examples of climate adaptation, suggesting a factual, informative purpose.

2. **Look for a Call to Action**: There is no direct suggestion for the reader to take action, which aligns with an informative rather than persuasive approach.

3. **Assess the Author's Purpose**: Here, the author's purpose is likely to inform readers about climate adaptation efforts in response to unpredictable weather.

Comprehensive Example Analysis

Now, let's apply these concepts to analyze a passage in detail:

Sample Passage: "In the rush to embrace artificial intelligence, many overlook the potential downsides of its rapid integration into society. From privacy concerns to job displacement, AI presents real risks that should not be ignored. Yet, its proponents argue that the benefits—such as efficiency and innovation—outweigh these concerns. As AI continues to shape the future, a balanced approach is essential to address both its promise and its pitfalls."

1. **Main Idea:**

    o   **Analyze Core Sentences**: Both the opening and concluding sentences mention "AI's rapid integration" and "a balanced approach."

    o   **Identify Repetition**: Terms like "risks," "benefits," and "balanced approach" highlight a dual perspective on AI.

    o   **Summarize Main Idea**: The main idea is that while AI has both significant benefits and risks, a balanced approach is essential for responsible integration.

2. **Tone:**

    o   **Examine Word Choices**: Phrases like "potential downsides," "risks that should not be ignored," and "balanced approach" suggest a cautious tone.

    o   **Identify Rhetorical Devices**: The author presents both sides of the argument, showing a thoughtful and measured tone rather than enthusiastic or fearful.

    o   **Determine Tone**: The tone is cautious and balanced, as the author addresses both positive and negative aspects of AI.

3. **Purpose:**

    o   **Consider Evidence Presented**: The author lists both risks and benefits, indicating a comprehensive, informative purpose.

    o   **Look for a Call to Action**: The suggestion for "a balanced approach" hints at an implicit recommendation, though not a direct call to action.

    o   **Determine Purpose**: The author's purpose is to inform readers about the complexities of AI's role in society, highlighting both risks and benefits to promote a balanced view.

By mastering these techniques for identifying the main idea, tone, and purpose, you'll not only enhance your comprehension but also improve your ability to tackle specific question types on the SAT. Regular practice with these strategies will help you read actively and respond to the subtleties of any passage, making you a more confident and analytical reader.

Breaking Down Complex Sentences to Understand Difficult Passages: A Detailed Guide

Complex sentences in SAT reading passages often contain layers of information packed with technical terms, nuanced ideas, and multiple clauses. These sentences are designed to challenge your comprehension by blending main points with additional details. Breaking them down systematically can reveal the author's core message without getting overwhelmed. Here's an expanded guide on how to approach these sentences, with advanced techniques and additional examples to deepen your understanding.

Why Breaking Down Complex Sentences Is Essential

Long and intricate sentences are common in SAT passages, particularly in science and history genres, where ideas often build on each other. Breaking down complex sentences helps you:

- **Identify the primary message** while recognizing secondary information.

- **Clarify relationships** between ideas, such as cause and effect or contrast.

- **Improve focus on the main argument** without getting sidetracked by excessive details.

With practice, breaking down sentences becomes a tool to demystify dense information and find the most important details quickly.

Step-by-Step Process for Breaking Down Complex Sentences

1. **Identify Clauses and Phrases**: Break the sentence into parts by locating independent and dependent clauses. The independent clause

typically conveys the main idea, while dependent clauses add context or supporting information. Recognizing each type of clause is essential because it helps you understand what's central versus supplementary.

- o **Independent Clauses**: These stand alone as complete ideas and often carry the sentence's main message.

- o **Dependent Clauses**: These add information but cannot stand alone. They often begin with words like "while," "because," "although," or "since."

Example: *"Although many view technology as a tool for progress, it can also create unexpected challenges, particularly in developing societies."*

- o **Independent Clause**: "It can also create unexpected challenges."

- o **Dependent Clause**: "Although many view technology as a tool for progress."

- o **Additional Phrase**: "particularly in developing societies" (specifying where challenges are felt most).

By distinguishing the independent clause, we see that the author's main point is the potential for technology to create challenges, with "progress" introduced as a contrasting perspective.

2. **Simplify Vocabulary**: Replace difficult or technical terms with simpler words or synonyms. This helps you focus on the sentence's core meaning rather than getting bogged down by complex language.

- o **Technique**: Mentally swap out complex words with simpler equivalents, especially when you encounter unfamiliar terms.

- o **Tip**: Use context clues to infer the meaning of complex words if you're unsure of their definitions.

Example: *"The proliferation of artificial intelligence across various industries has sparked both excitement and trepidation among experts and consumers alike."*

- o Simplify "proliferation" to "spread."

- o Replace "trepidation" with "worry" or "concern."

      o   Simplified sentence: "The spread of artificial intelligence in many industries has caused excitement and worry among experts and consumers."

By simplifying vocabulary, the sentence becomes easier to process and understand in context.

3. **Paraphrase in Your Own Words**: Rewrite the sentence in simpler terms to ensure that you've understood it. Paraphrasing forces you to interpret the sentence's meaning rather than simply reading it passively.

      o   **Technique**: Summarize the main idea and essential details, stripping the sentence down to its core.

      o   **Tip**: Focus on the main message conveyed by the independent clause, then add key details from dependent clauses if they contribute essential context.

Example: *Original Sentence*: "While early studies on gene editing suggest transformative medical applications, ethical concerns and regulatory hurdles remain significant."

      o   **Main Clause**: "Ethical concerns and regulatory hurdles remain significant."

      o   **Supporting Clause**: "While early studies on gene editing suggest transformative medical applications."

      o   **Paraphrased Sentence**: "Gene editing could greatly impact medicine, but ethical and legal issues are still big obstacles."

Paraphrasing this sentence makes it more accessible and provides a clear takeaway: gene editing holds promise, but ethical and regulatory issues complicate its adoption.

Advanced Techniques for Complex Sentences

For particularly challenging sentences, use these additional strategies to deepen your understanding:

1. **Look for Transitional Words and Phrases**: Transitions often signal relationships between clauses, like contrast, cause and effect, or

emphasis. Understanding these relationships clarifies the structure of the sentence and the relationship between ideas.

- o **Contrast Words**: "However," "although," "but" (signal opposition).

- o **Cause and Effect Words**: "Because," "therefore," "as a result" (indicate causation).

- o **Emphasis Words**: "Indeed," "in fact," "notably" (highlight importance).

Example: *"While advancements in renewable energy are indeed promising, significant challenges, such as high costs and infrastructure limitations, must be addressed to achieve widespread adoption."*

- o "While" introduces contrast, suggesting that although progress is positive, issues remain.

- o "Indeed" emphasizes the positive aspect of advancements.

- o Main message: "Renewable energy shows potential, but obstacles like cost and infrastructure prevent full adoption."

2. **Separate Lists or Series of Details**: Complex sentences often include lists of examples or reasons, separated by commas or semi-colons. Breaking these lists into individual items clarifies the types of support or evidence the author provides.

- o **Technique**: Mentally or visually divide the list into bullet points to see each component more clearly.

- o **Tip**: Focus on how each list item connects to the main clause or idea.

Example: *"The advantages of solar energy—its renewability, low environmental impact, and potential to reduce reliance on fossil fuels—make it an attractive alternative for future power generation."*

- o **List:**

  - Renewability

  - Low environmental impact

  - Potential to reduce fossil fuel reliance

- o **Main Idea**: Solar energy's benefits make it a promising alternative for energy production.

By separating these elements, you can more easily see how each advantage supports the overall argument in favor of solar energy.

3. **Apply the "Core Message Test"**: After breaking down and simplifying a sentence, ask yourself, "What is the author ultimately trying to convey?" This test helps confirm whether your interpretation aligns with the author's intended message.

Example: *"Despite the widespread adoption of electric vehicles as a sustainable solution, concerns about battery disposal and energy consumption during manufacturing continue to provoke debate within environmental circles."*

- o **Core Message Test**: What's the essential idea? The primary message is that although electric vehicles are generally seen as sustainable, there are still environmental concerns.

- o **Core Message Summary**: Electric vehicles are popular for sustainability, but issues like battery waste and manufacturing impact remain debated.

By using the "Core Message Test," you're verifying your understanding of the sentence and ensuring that you haven't missed any crucial details.

Practice Application: Complex Sentence Breakdown

Sample Sentence:
"Although remote work has provided flexibility for employees, concerns about decreased collaboration, isolation, and potential declines in productivity remain prevalent in many organizations."

Step-by-Step Breakdown:

1. **Identify Clauses**:

   - o Independent Clause: "Concerns about decreased collaboration, isolation, and potential declines in productivity remain prevalent in many organizations."

   - o Dependent Clause: "Although remote work has provided flexibility for employees."

2. **Simplify Vocabulary**:

- o   "Decreased collaboration" → "less teamwork"

- o   "Isolation" → "feeling alone"

- o   "Potential declines in productivity" → "lower productivity"

3. **Paraphrase**:

- o   Simplified sentence: "Even though remote work is flexible, many organizations worry about less teamwork, isolation, and productivity."

4. **Core Message Test**:

- o   The author is suggesting that remote work has benefits, like flexibility, but also raises concerns in organizations about teamwork and productivity.

Breaking down sentences in this way not only clarifies meaning but also reinforces comprehension, helping you tackle even the most challenging SAT passages with ease. Regular practice with these techniques will improve your reading efficiency and accuracy, making it easier to answer related questions quickly and confidently.

Challenge Yourself: Try Active Reading on a Sample Passage

Sample Passage:
"Anna's admiration for her grandfather grew each time she learned more about his contributions to the community. Although he was often away, volunteering with different organizations, he always made sure to set time aside for family, instilling in her the values of kindness and dedication."

Practice Task:

1. **Annotate**:

- o   **Underline** or **highlight** key phrases that capture the passage's main ideas.

- o   **Circle** any names, terms, or values that might be important for understanding the author's perspective.

2. **Analyze for Main Idea, Tone, and Purpose**:

- o   What do you think the **main idea** of this passage is?

    o   How would you describe the **author's tone**?

    o   What might be the **purpose** of including these details about Anna's grandfather?

Suggested Answers:

- **Main Idea**: Anna's grandfather's dedication to community and family has greatly influenced her values.

- **Tone**: Respectful and admiring.

- **Purpose**: To highlight the positive impact of family role models on character development.

Reflection Prompt: As you work through these techniques, take a moment to consider how each step helps you understand the text better. Do you find that annotation improves your focus, or that breaking down complex sentences makes it easier to retain information? Reflection on your methods can reinforce effective habits and highlight areas for growth.

Through repeated practice and applying these active reading strategies to each passage type, you'll build the skills needed to approach the Digital SAT Reading section with confidence and insight.

4.3 Tackling Evidence-Based Reading Questions

Evidence-based questions are a cornerstone of the Digital SAT Reading section. They require not only selecting the correct answer but also identifying the part of the text that supports it. Mastering these questions takes practice and a strategic approach. In this subsection, you'll learn effective methods for identifying and selecting the best evidence, avoiding common pitfalls, and answering with confidence.

Understanding Evidence-Based Questions: Deep Dive into the Pair Structure

In the Digital SAT Reading section, evidence-based questions require more than simply finding the correct answer to a question—they require you to back up your answer with specific lines from the text. This unique structure challenges you to be both analytical and precise, assessing not only your comprehension of the material but also your ability to justify your understanding with textual evidence.

Let's break down how this pair structure works and why it's so essential to SAT success. I'll also provide more advanced techniques and examples to help you master this question type.

The Structure of Evidence-Based Questions

Evidence-based questions appear in two parts that are designed to work together:

1. **Primary Question**: This question prompts you to analyze the passage and answer a query about its content. It might ask you to infer the author's intent, determine a character's feelings, or identify the passage's main idea.

2. **Follow-Up Evidence Question**: The evidence question directly follows the primary question and provides multiple line references. You are asked to choose the line(s) that best support the answer you selected for the primary question.

The pairing of these questions is intentional. It's a test of your ability to:

- **Interpret the Text Correctly**: Select an accurate answer based on your understanding.

- **Justify Your Interpretation**: Identify specific text that supports your interpretation, demonstrating that your answer is based on evidence rather than assumption or guesswork.

This approach is effective for assessing your reading comprehension skills at a higher level, as it requires you to go beyond a simple "correct answer" and connect your choice directly to the text.

Why the Pair Structure Is Important

The evidence-based question structure serves several critical functions in assessing reading comprehension:

- **Ensures Answer Accuracy**: By requiring evidence, the SAT Reading section minimizes the likelihood of "educated guesses." If your answer to the primary question lacks strong evidence, it's an indication that you may need to reevaluate.

- **Encourages Textual Precision**: This format emphasizes the importance of paying close attention to the text. You must be precise about where in the passage the supporting information is located, helping develop your skill in citing and interpreting specific parts of a passage.

- **Builds Analytical Skills**: Evidence-based questions train you to think analytically, examining how different parts of a text contribute to its overall meaning. You learn to connect individual lines with broader ideas, which is invaluable for academic reading and analysis.

Advanced Techniques for Tackling Evidence-Based Question Pairs

Let's explore a step-by-step approach, as well as advanced strategies for mastering this question type.

1. **Read the Primary Question Carefully**:
   Before diving into the passage or answer choices, focus intently on what the primary question is asking. Is it looking for an inference, a character's feelings, or a specific detail? Try to get a clear sense of the kind of information the question seeks. This initial clarity will guide you in locating the correct evidence.

Example: If the primary question asks, "What can be inferred about the author's view on technology?" you'll know to look for words or phrases that reveal opinion—like "beneficial," "concerning," or "potential"—rather than factual descriptions.

2. **Form a Mental Hypothesis**: As you read the passage, try to form a preliminary answer to the primary question in your mind. Having this hypothesis before examining the evidence choices will allow you to search the passage more purposefully.

3. **Identify Potential Evidence**: Skim through the passage and note any sections that might contain relevant information. For instance, if the primary question asks about a character's motivation, look for lines where the character's thoughts, feelings, or actions are discussed.

4. **Answer the Primary Question First (Without Looking at the Evidence Choices):**
   Try to answer the primary question on your own before reading the evidence choices. This way, you're less likely to be swayed by evidence options that may seem relevant but don't actually support the correct answer.

5. **Evaluate Each Evidence Option Carefully:**
   After selecting an answer to the primary question, read each evidence choice and consider whether it truly supports your response. Be cautious of evidence that appears relevant but lacks a direct connection to the question's focus.

6. **Verify the Direct Relationship Between Answer and Evidence:**
   Finally, confirm that your selected evidence option directly supports the primary answer. If the evidence doesn't clearly reinforce the idea behind your answer, reevaluate your choices. This step is critical, as it prevents you from choosing evidence based on assumption rather than logical support.

Detailed Example: Evidence-Based Question in Action

Sample Passage: "Clara stared at the city skyline, feeling a surge of excitement mixed with trepidation. She had always dreamed of living in a bustling city, yet the towering buildings and relentless noise made her long for the quiet streets of her hometown. Still, she reminded herself of her goals and resolved to embrace this new chapter, no matter the challenges."

Primary Question: What can be inferred about Clara's attitude toward moving to the city?

- **Answer Choices:**

  - (A) She feels entirely optimistic about the move.

  - (B) She is uncertain but determined to succeed.

  - (C) She regrets her decision to move.

  - (D) She is indifferent to her new environment.

Evidence Question: Which line provides the best evidence for the previous answer?

- **Evidence Choices:**

  - (A) "Clara stared at the city skyline, feeling a surge of excitement mixed with trepidation."

  - (B) "She had always dreamed of living in a bustling city."

  - (C) "The towering buildings and relentless noise made her long for the quiet streets of her hometown."

  - (D) "She reminded herself of her goals and resolved to embrace this new chapter."

Step-by-Step Walkthrough:

1. **Read the Primary Question Carefully:** The question asks for an inference about Clara's feelings toward the move. Words like "attitude," "uncertain," and "determined" indicate that we need to understand her emotional reaction and outlook on her new life in the city.

2. **Form a Hypothesis:** From the passage, it's clear that Clara feels a mix of excitement and trepidation. She also reflects on her goals and "resolves to embrace this new chapter." This suggests determination tempered by some hesitation.

3. **Select the Primary Answer:** Based on the above hypothesis, (B) "She is uncertain but determined to succeed" is the most accurate choice, capturing both her ambivalence and resolve.

4. **Examine the Evidence Choices:**

   - **(A)** highlights "excitement mixed with trepidation," which aligns with her mixed feelings.

   - **(B)** mentions her dream of city life, which hints at her motivation but doesn't directly confirm her attitude toward the move.

   - **(C)** suggests nostalgia for her hometown, but it doesn't provide evidence of her determination to stay.

   - **(D)** "She reminded herself of her goals and resolved to embrace this new chapter" directly supports her determination, making it the best choice.

5. **Verify the Direct Connection**: Option (D) is the only choice that reflects Clara's resolve and her intent to embrace the challenges ahead. This evidence best supports the answer (B) because it shows her determination to adapt, even though she has mixed emotions.

Final Answer Pair:

- **Primary Question Answer**: (B) She is uncertain but determined to succeed.

- **Evidence Question Answer**: (D) "She reminded herself of her goals and resolved to embrace this new chapter."

Practice Exercise: Test Your Skills

Try answering this sample question set on your own to reinforce your understanding.

Sample Passage:
"While many praised the new educational reforms for their innovative approach, others feared the rapid changes would overwhelm teachers and disrupt students' learning routines. The debate grew as more educators voiced their concerns about the policy's sustainability."

Primary Question: What can be inferred about the public's reaction to the new educational reforms?

- **Answer Choices**:

    o (A) The public is universally supportive of the reforms.

    o (B) Some people have concerns about the reforms' impact on education.

    o (C) Most people are indifferent to the new reforms.

    o (D) The public is opposed to any educational changes.

Evidence Question: Which line provides the best evidence for the previous answer?

- **Evidence Choices**:

    o (A) "Many praised the new educational reforms for their innovative approach."

- (B) "Others feared the rapid changes would overwhelm teachers and disrupt students' learning routines."

- (C) "The debate grew as more educators voiced their concerns."

- (D) "The policy's sustainability was questioned by some."

Suggested Answer:

- **Primary Question Answer:** (B) Some people have concerns about the reforms' impact on education.

- **Evidence Question Answer:** (B) "Others feared the rapid changes would overwhelm teachers and disrupt students' learning routines."

Step-by-Step Strategy for Answering Evidence-Based Questions

1. Read the Primary Question Carefully

Purpose: The primary question sets the direction for your analysis. By reading it carefully, you ensure that you fully understand what the question is asking and which part of the passage you should focus on.

Advanced Techniques:

- **Identify the Type of Information Needed:** Evidence-based questions can ask for a main idea, inference, or specific detail. Recognizing the type of question helps you zero in on the kind of information required:

  - **Main Idea Questions:** Look for overarching themes or arguments.

  - **Inference Questions:** Consider underlying meanings, implied emotions, or perspectives.

  - **Detail Questions:** Focus on specific data points, dates, or concrete information provided in the passage.

- **Highlight Keywords in the Question:** Identify keywords or phrases in the question that specify what to focus on. For example, in a question like, "What is the author's attitude toward urbanization?" keywords are "author's attitude" and "urbanization." These words direct you to look for tone indicators and opinions regarding urbanization, which you can identify through descriptive language, opinions, and judgments.

Example: If the primary question is, "What can be inferred about the narrator's relationship with their family?" the keywords are "inferred" and "relationship with their family." You now know you're looking for implicit information (not directly stated) that hints at the narrator's emotions, interactions, or underlying feelings toward their family.

2. Scan the Passage and Anticipate Evidence

Purpose: Scanning the passage for potential evidence before diving into the answer choices keeps you grounded in the text rather than being led astray by answer options that "sound right" but aren't supported by the passage.

Advanced Techniques:

- **Use Structural Cues in the Passage**: Passages often have a predictable structure. Authors may introduce ideas in the beginning, develop them in the middle, and conclude with a summarizing or reflective statement. Anticipate that evidence for main ideas or summaries will likely be found in the introduction or conclusion, while specific details or examples are often located in the middle sections.

- **Look for "Hot Spots" Based on the Question Type**:

    o **Attitude or Tone Questions**: Look for adjectives, adverbs, or any emotionally charged language.

    o **Inference Questions**: Pay attention to descriptive phrases, dialogue, or actions that suggest feelings, attitudes, or implications.

    o **Specific Detail Questions**: Identify paragraphs with factual data, dates, or events that could answer specific questions.

Example: In a passage where the author describes a controversial environmental policy, an attitude question might prompt you to scan for words like "progressive," "harmful," or "essential." If these tone words appear in the introductory paragraph, they may indicate the author's overall stance, while specific arguments or counterarguments will likely be expanded on in subsequent paragraphs.

3. Answer the Primary Question First (Without Looking at the Evidence Choices)

Purpose: Answering the question independently reinforces your understanding of the text and helps you avoid being influenced by evidence choices that may seem to fit but are not fully aligned with the correct answer.

Advanced Techniques:

- **Formulate a Brief Answer in Your Own Words**: Summarize your answer in a few words. This prevents you from overanalyzing and keeps your answer grounded in the main idea.

- **Rely on Contextual Memory**: After reading the passage, you'll often have a mental "snapshot" of the areas where certain ideas were discussed. Relying on this contextual memory can lead you to parts of the text that reinforce your answer.

- **Visualize Answer Possibilities**: Imagine a few possible answers for the primary question based on your interpretation of the text. For example, if the question is about the author's opinion, consider if the answer might lean toward positive, negative, or neutral. This can prepare you to identify the best answer once you review the options.

Example: Suppose the question asks, "How does the narrator feel about his new job?" Based on a quick scan of the text, you might answer "ambivalent" in your own words, noting that he seems to appreciate certain aspects but has reservations about others. Having this preliminary answer makes it easier to choose the option that best aligns with this understanding.

4. Select the Evidence that Best Matches Your Answer

Purpose: By carefully reviewing the evidence options, you can identify the text that most directly supports your answer without unrelated details.

Advanced Techniques:

- **Focus on Exact Language Alignment**: Choose the evidence that directly uses language or ideas from your primary answer. Look for words, phrases, or concepts in the evidence that match or echo your answer choice.

- **Eliminate "Partially Correct" Evidence**: Evidence options may include statements that seem related but don't fully capture the answer. Discard any choice that only touches on part of your answer. Evidence must support the primary answer in full.

- **Assess the Completeness of Each Option**: Good evidence will directly relate to the full context of the question and answer. Be cautious of evidence that addresses part of your answer but leaves out essential elements.

Example: If your answer to a question about the narrator's experience in a foreign city is "nostalgic yet hopeful," you'll want evidence that captures both aspects, not just one. Look for an option that shows both feelings—perhaps a line where the narrator reflects on memories while mentioning their excitement for the future.

5. Double-Check the Connection

Purpose: Verifying the connection between the primary answer and evidence ensures that your choices are logically aligned and rooted in the text.

Advanced Techniques:

- **Rephrase the Connection in Your Own Words**: After selecting your evidence, explain to yourself how it supports the answer. This step often reveals if the evidence is genuinely aligned or if it's a near miss.

- **Ask "Why" the Evidence Supports the Answer**: By asking "why" the chosen evidence is correct, you reinforce the logic of your choice. This step is particularly helpful if the answer or evidence seems too implicit or abstract.

- **Use a Process of Elimination for Evidence Options**: If you're uncertain, systematically eliminate evidence choices that don't fully match. Ruling out weaker options increases the likelihood of selecting the most precise evidence.

Example Walkthrough: Let's walk through a sample question to demonstrate how this final step looks in practice.

Sample Passage:
"Though Benjamin appreciated the convenience of digital communication, he often found himself missing the depth of face-to-face conversations. Messages could be misunderstood, or feelings lost in translation, leaving him feeling disconnected even as he communicated constantly."

Primary Question: What can be inferred about Benjamin's feelings toward digital communication?

- **Answer Choices**:

    o   (A) He finds it preferable to in-person conversations.

    o   (B) He feels disconnected despite the convenience.

    o   (C) He avoids it whenever possible.

    o   (D) He believes it is superior for expressing emotions.

Selected Primary Answer: (B) He feels disconnected despite the convenience.

Evidence Question: Which line provides the best evidence for the previous answer?

- **Evidence Choices**:

    o   (A) "Benjamin appreciated the convenience of digital communication."

    o   (B) "He often found himself missing the depth of face-to-face conversations."

    o   (C) "Messages could be misunderstood, or feelings lost in translation."

    o   (D) "Leaving him feeling disconnected even as he communicated constantly."

Analysis and Double-Check:

1. **Assess Completeness**: Evidence (D) most fully captures Benjamin's feelings of disconnection, supporting answer (B) with the specific mention of feeling "disconnected."

2. **Eliminate Partial Matches**: While (B) and (C) touch on relevant themes, only (D) combines both convenience and disconnection, making it the strongest choice.

3. **Final Connection**: Evidence (D) fully reinforces that Benjamin feels disconnected even as he uses digital communication for its convenience. This alignment confirms that both the primary answer and evidence choice are well-matched.

Avoiding Common Pitfalls in Evidence-Based Questions: A Detailed Guide

Evidence-based questions are challenging not just because they require two steps—finding the correct answer and supporting evidence—but also because they're full of traps designed to mislead test-takers. Being aware of these pitfalls is crucial for selecting precise, relevant evidence. Let's go deeper into each common pitfall, explore why they're misleading, and provide strategies to avoid them.

---

1. Beware of Irrelevant Evidence

Irrelevant evidence is one of the most common traps in evidence-based questions. These choices often appear connected to the topic but fail to support the specific answer to the primary question.

Why This Pitfall is Misleading:

Irrelevant evidence options are designed to look appealing because they:

- **Match the Theme or Topic**: They may discuss the same broad subject as the question but fail to connect directly to the specific answer.

- **Contain Familiar Keywords**: Some evidence options include keywords from the primary question or other parts of the passage, tricking test-takers into thinking they're relevant.

Strategy to Avoid Irrelevant Evidence:

- **Align with the Answer's Core Idea**: Once you select an answer for the primary question, identify its core idea (e.g., a character's emotion or a specific event). Only choose evidence that clearly reinforces this idea, not just the general theme of the passage.

- **Ask "Does This Evidence Add to My Answer?"**: For example, if the answer involves a character's "reluctance," don't settle for evidence that merely describes the character's actions or appearance without showing reluctance.

Example:

If the question is, "What can be inferred about the character's motivation?" and the answer is about the character's "hesitation," irrelevant evidence might describe what the character is doing without explaining why they're hesitant.

In this case, the right evidence should explicitly highlight signs of hesitation, like "uncertain glance" or "paused before acting," rather than just describing an action unrelated to motivation.

---

2. Avoid "Too Broad" or "Too Narrow" Evidence

Another common mistake is choosing evidence that's either too broad or too narrow to support the answer.

- **Too Broad**: Evidence that's too general might address the passage's overall theme but lacks the focus necessary to support a specific detail in the primary answer.

- **Too Narrow**: Evidence that's too specific may address only one part of the primary answer, failing to capture the full scope required.

Why This Pitfall is Misleading:

Evidence options that are too broad or too narrow can easily be mistaken for correct answers because they seem relevant in isolation. However:

- **Broad Evidence** often lacks the specificity needed for detailed questions, like questions asking for a character's exact feelings or motivations.

- **Narrow Evidence** may only partially address the question, leading to an incomplete or even incorrect answer.

Strategy to Avoid Broad/Narrow Evidence:

- **Define the Scope of the Primary Answer**: Before reviewing evidence, ask, "Is the primary answer addressing a specific detail, a general statement, or a nuanced emotion?" Then, use this scope to filter out options that don't match.

- **Look for Precise Language**: If the question is specific, select evidence that includes precise language or details. For general questions, choose broader statements that capture the passage's overall theme.

Example:

If the primary question asks, "What does the author imply about the impact of pollution on marine life?" and the answer discusses a specific effect on coral reefs, evidence that broadly talks about pollution's impact on all ecosystems is too broad. Instead, look for evidence focusing specifically on marine ecosystems or coral reefs to match the specific detail.

---

3. Don't Rely on Your Memory of the Passage

Memory can play tricks on us, especially when passages contain dense information or complex arguments. Relying on memory alone often leads to selecting evidence that "sounds right" but doesn't actually support the chosen answer when revisited in the text.

Why This Pitfall is Misleading:

- **Memory Bias**: We tend to remember certain parts of the passage more vividly, especially the beginning or end, and may incorrectly assume these sections contain the evidence we need.

- **False Familiarity**: When an evidence option feels "familiar," it's easy to mistake it for the right choice, even if it's only loosely related.

Strategy to Avoid Memory Traps:

- **Always Double-Check in the Text**: After choosing an answer, go back to the passage to confirm the supporting evidence. This ensures your choice is based on the actual content rather than memory.

- **Cross-Reference with the Primary Answer**: Revisit the part of the passage you believe contains the answer and double-check that it clearly supports the primary answer.

Example:

If the primary question asks about a character's feelings in the final paragraph, don't rely on your memory of earlier details about the character's personality. Instead, go directly to the final paragraph to locate the specific line(s) that reveal their feelings.

---

4. Practice Elimination

Ruling out incorrect options is just as important as selecting the correct one. Incorrect evidence choices can be tempting, especially when they include elements that appear relevant. Systematically eliminating poor choices helps narrow down the options and makes it easier to identify the best match.

Why This Pitfall is Misleading:

- **Distractor Options**: The SAT includes distractor choices that seem plausible but contain subtle inaccuracies or incomplete information.

- **Similarity to Correct Evidence**: Some evidence choices will be close but not quite right, containing ideas that seem relevant without fully supporting the answer.

Strategy to Practice Effective Elimination:

- **Identify and Reject Mismatched Options**: Evidence that doesn't align directly with the core idea in the primary answer should be ruled out immediately.

- **Mark and Compare Remaining Options**: After eliminating obvious mismatches, review the remaining choices and compare them to determine which best supports the primary answer. Look for differences in how precisely each option relates to the core idea.

Example Walkthrough:

Sample Passage:
"Despite her achievements, Lila often felt unfulfilled. She was proud of her career success, but a lingering sense of something missing weighed heavily on her. As her friends celebrated her recent promotion, she found herself wondering if this was truly the life she wanted."

Primary Question: What can be inferred about Lila's feelings toward her career success?

- **Answer Choices**:

  o (A) She feels completely satisfied with her achievements.

  o (B) She feels proud but uncertain if it's what she truly wants.

  o (C) She regrets her career choices entirely.

  o (D) She is indifferent to her career success.

Selected Primary Answer: (B) She feels proud but uncertain if it's what she truly wants.

Evidence Question: Which line provides the best evidence for the previous answer?

- **Evidence Choices**:

    o (A) "Despite her achievements, Lila often felt unfulfilled."

    o (B) "She was proud of her career success."

    o (C) "A lingering sense of something missing weighed heavily on her."

    o (D) "She found herself wondering if this was truly the life she wanted."

Step-by-Step Elimination and Final Choice:

1. **Identify Irrelevant Evidence**:

    o Option (B), "She was proud of her career success," addresses only her pride, missing her uncertainty. Eliminate it as "too narrow."

2. **Filter Out Overly Broad Evidence**:

    o Option (A), "Despite her achievements, Lila often felt unfulfilled," is too general. It hints at her feelings but lacks specific language that captures her mixed pride and uncertainty.

3. **Select the Best Evidence**:

    o Option (D), "She found herself wondering if this was truly the life she wanted," fully aligns with the chosen answer by capturing both her doubt and reflection on her life choices.

4. **Confirm and Verify**:

    o After elimination, option (D) clearly supports answer (B) without irrelevant details, making it the best evidence.

Through systematic elimination, the correct evidence becomes more apparent, reducing the chance of choosing a plausible yet incorrect option.

Challenge Yourself: Expanded Practice Set

In this expanded practice challenge, we'll focus on analyzing each aspect of the evidence-based question more thoroughly. You'll start by reading the passage and primary question, then follow a step-by-step breakdown to help solidify the reasoning behind each answer choice. Let's go!

Sample Passage:

"James stood at the edge of the cliff, feeling both exhilarated and apprehensive as he looked out over the sprawling forest below. He had spent years preparing for this moment, but now, with the world stretched out beneath him, he questioned if he was truly ready."

Step 1: Analyze the Primary Question

Primary Question: What does the passage suggest about James's feelings at this moment?

Answer Choices:

- (A) He feels completely confident.

- (B) He is uncertain despite his preparation.

- (C) He regrets his preparation.

- (D) He is uninterested in the view below.

Instructions:

- **Highlight Keywords** in the question: In this case, "James's feelings" and "at this moment" are important. This means we're focusing on his emotional state as described in this specific moment in the passage.

- **Identify the Type of Question**: This is an inference question, as it's asking us to deduce James's feelings based on his actions and thoughts.

Step 2: Formulate a Preliminary Answer for the Primary Question

Task: Before looking at the answer choices in detail, try to summarize James's emotional state based on your reading of the passage.

Key Observations:

- James feels a mix of emotions: **exhilaration** and **apprehension**.

- Despite his preparation, he **questions** his readiness, which implies uncertainty.

Preliminary Answer: James feels both excited and uncertain about this moment.

Step 3: Evaluate Each Answer Choice

Instructions: For each answer choice, evaluate whether it matches your preliminary answer. Consider the specific language used in each option and compare it to your understanding of the passage.

- **(A) He feels completely confident:** This option is inaccurate, as "completely confident" doesn't align with his "apprehensive" and uncertain state. Eliminate (A).

- **(B) He is uncertain despite his preparation:** This option matches the text's description of James's mixed feelings, particularly his questioning of whether he is "truly ready." (B) is a strong contender.

- **(C) He regrets his preparation:** There's no indication in the text that James regrets his preparation; he only questions his readiness, not the decision itself. Eliminate (C).

- **(D) He is uninterested in the view below:** James's feelings include exhilaration as he takes in the view, which shows interest rather than disinterest. Eliminate (D).

Primary Answer: (B) - "He is uncertain despite his preparation."

Step 4: Analyze the Evidence Question

Evidence Question: Which line provides the best evidence for the previous answer?

Evidence Choices:

- (A) "Feeling both exhilarated and apprehensive."

- (B) "He had spent years preparing for this moment."

103

- (C) "With the world stretched out beneath him."

- (D) "He questioned if he was truly ready."

Instructions:

1. **Identify the Core of the Primary Answer**: The primary answer centers on James's **uncertainty** despite his **preparation**. Look for evidence that confirms both of these points.

2. **Evaluate Each Evidence Choice**: Examine how each choice supports or fails to support the primary answer.

- **(A) "Feeling both exhilarated and apprehensive."**

  o This choice touches on his emotions but doesn't specifically confirm his **uncertainty** about being ready. It's relevant but lacks the focus needed to fully support the primary answer. Eliminate (A).

- **(B) "He had spent years preparing for this moment."**

  o While this line confirms his preparation, it doesn't reflect his uncertainty. It provides context but doesn't directly support his mixed feelings. Eliminate (B).

- **(C) "With the world stretched out beneath him."**

  o This line describes the setting but doesn't give insight into James's feelings or readiness. Eliminate (C).

- **(D) "He questioned if he was truly ready."**

  o This line directly shows his uncertainty, which aligns perfectly with the primary answer's focus on his self-doubt. This is the best evidence choice.

Best Evidence: (D) - "He questioned if he was truly ready."

Explanation and Reflection

Final Answer Pair:

- **Primary Answer:** (B) - He is uncertain despite his preparation.

- **Evidence Answer:** (D) - "He questioned if he was truly ready."

Explanation: James's mixed feelings are best captured by answer (B) because the passage explicitly describes him feeling both excitement and apprehension. Evidence choice (D) directly reflects his uncertainty and reinforces the idea that, despite his preparation, he's unsure about his readiness.

Extended Challenge: Self-Reflection Questions

To strengthen your skills, reflect on the following:

1. **Why was it important to eliminate choices (A), (C), and (D) for the primary question?**
   Consider how these choices fail to capture James's complex emotions or misinterpret his feelings.

2. **How did you determine that evidence option (D) was superior to (A), even though both mention feelings?**
   Reflect on why specific phrases, such as "questioned if he was truly ready," provided a clearer connection to the primary answer.

3. **What part of this process felt challenging, and why?**
   Identifying areas where you hesitated can help you recognize where to focus future practice.

4. **How did defining the question type help guide your approach?**
   Thinking about how identifying an inference question shaped your approach can reinforce the importance of recognizing question types on the SAT.

Additional Practice: Apply to a New Sample

Try these steps with a different passage to further reinforce your understanding.

Sample Passage:
"Ella had always loved the ocean, but today, as she stood on the shore watching the storm roll in, she felt an unfamiliar sense of dread. The waves crashed more fiercely than ever, and the sky seemed darker, more ominous. She clutched her coat tightly, bracing herself for the oncoming storm."

Primary Question: What does the passage suggest about Ella's feelings toward the ocean at this moment?

- **Answer Choices:**

    o (A) She feels at peace despite the storm.

    o (B) She is afraid of the storm's intensity.

    o (C) She is excited by the powerful waves.

    o (D) She is indifferent to the approaching storm.

Evidence Question: Which line provides the best evidence for the previous answer?

- **Evidence Choices:**

    o (A) "Ella had always loved the ocean."

    o (B) "She felt an unfamiliar sense of dread."

    o (C) "The waves crashed more fiercely than ever."

    o (D) "She clutched her coat tightly, bracing herself."

Steps:

1. Analyze the primary question, identifying keywords and defining the question type.

2. Formulate a preliminary answer before reviewing choices.

3. Evaluate each answer choice for accuracy.

4. Select the best evidence that directly supports your chosen answer.

This expanded challenge helps solidify your approach to evidence-based questions, sharpening your ability to analyze and select precise evidence. Practicing these steps regularly will increase your confidence and accuracy with complex reading questions on the SAT.

Final Reflection: Building Confidence with Evidence-Based Questions

By applying these strategies consistently, you'll find that evidence-based questions become more approachable. These techniques are designed to help you read actively, analyze logically, and feel reassured in your answers. As you practice, remember: every question is an opportunity to strengthen your analytical skills, one answer at a time.

4.4 Practicing with Reading Comprehension Exercises

In this section, you'll learn how to elevate your reading comprehension skills through targeted exercises, timed drills, and realistic SAT practice simulations. These strategies are designed to help you build speed, accuracy, and confidence, ensuring you're well-prepared to tackle the SAT Reading section.

We'll cover:

- How to use timed drills effectively to build your reading speed and comprehension.

- Detailed practice exercises tailored to each SAT question type.

- Techniques for creating a realistic SAT testing environment to reduce anxiety and improve performance.

By approaching your practice sessions methodically, you'll gain the stamina, focus, and strategic insights needed to excel on test day.

Using Timed Reading Drills to Build Speed and Accuracy

Timed reading drills are essential for developing the ability to work under pressure, improving your reading speed, and ensuring accurate comprehension. With consistent practice, timed drills help build the resilience you'll need to maintain focus through the entire SAT Reading section.

Step-by-Step Guide to Timed Reading Drills

1. **Start with a Baseline**
   Begin by reading a passage without any time constraints, just to see how long it naturally takes you to read and answer questions accurately. This initial exercise provides a baseline and allows you to pinpoint specific areas (such as inference or vocabulary questions) that may need extra focus.

2. **Set Realistic Time Goals**
   On the SAT, you should aim to answer questions for each passage in around 12-13 minutes. Start with a target time of 15 minutes, and as

you become more comfortable, reduce this gradually until you can complete each passage within the ideal time range.

3. **Practice Focused Attention**
    During your timed drill, make it a habit to practice "focused scanning," where you briefly scan the questions before reading the passage. This helps you identify what information to prioritize and increases your efficiency.

4. **Conduct a Post-Drill Analysis**
    After each drill, review your answers, noting which questions took the longest or led to mistakes. Analyze any patterns, such as frequently missed question types or particular passage topics that slow you down. This reflection builds awareness of areas that need improvement and reinforces your learning.

Practical Exercise: Timed Drill Example

Here's a short passage with a timed question. Set a timer for one minute and work to answer quickly and accurately.

Sample Passage:
"As Emma watched the children play in the park, she couldn't help but feel a pang of nostalgia. She remembered her own carefree days, filled with laughter and endless curiosity. Those were the days before life's demands set in, shaping her into the responsible adult she'd become."

Question: What can be inferred about Emma's current feelings toward her past?

- (A) She regrets her childhood.

- (B) She feels nostalgic about her carefree youth.

- (C) She is indifferent to her childhood memories.

- (D) She is glad to have moved on from childhood.

After completing the question, take a few seconds to reflect on your timing and confidence in your choice. Were there words or phrases in the passage that helped you make a quick decision? Practicing these quick reflections will reinforce your ability to work efficiently under timed conditions.

Detailed Practice Exercises for Each SAT Reading Question Type

Each question type in the SAT Reading section requires different skills. Mastering them individually through targeted exercises will improve both your accuracy and your comfort with the varied question styles on the SAT.

1. Inference Questions

Overview: Inference questions ask you to read between the lines, interpreting underlying ideas or emotions that aren't explicitly stated.

Targeted Exercise:
Sample Passage:
"Daniel's face was set in a thoughtful expression as he listened to the debate unfold around him. He rarely spoke up in such situations, preferring instead to listen and reflect before forming an opinion. Despite his silence, those who knew him well could sense the gears turning in his mind."

Question: What can be inferred about Daniel's approach to debates?

- (A) He avoids forming opinions.

- (B) He is highly opinionated.

- (C) He prefers to think carefully before speaking.

- (D) He dislikes listening to others' viewpoints.

Practice Insight: After selecting your answer, write a sentence explaining why the correct choice is the best fit. This helps reinforce the specific reasoning skills needed for inference questions, where direct answers are not provided, and you must rely on subtle context clues.

---

2. Evidence-Based Questions

Overview: Evidence-based questions ask you to choose the line or lines that support your answer to a primary question. This dual-question format tests both comprehension and the ability to justify your answer with specific text evidence.

Targeted Exercise:
Sample Passage:
"Leah loved her job at the animal shelter, but she couldn't ignore the emotional toll it took on her. Every adoption felt like a victory, yet each abandoned pet left her with a lingering sadness. Over time, she began to wonder if the highs and lows were sustainable."

Primary Question: How does Leah feel about her work at the shelter?

- (A) She finds it entirely rewarding.

- (B) She feels indifferent toward the animals.

- (C) She is torn between her love for the work and its emotional challenges.

- (D) She feels the work is meaningless.

Evidence Question: Which line best supports your answer?

- (A) "Leah loved her job at the animal shelter."

- (B) "Every adoption felt like a victory."

- (C) "Each abandoned pet left her with a lingering sadness."

- (D) "She began to wonder if the highs and lows were sustainable."

Reflective Task: After choosing the correct evidence, explain why each incorrect evidence option was insufficient or only partially relevant. This practice builds precision, helping you eliminate answer choices effectively on test day.

---

3. Vocabulary-in-Context Questions

Overview: Vocabulary-in-context questions require you to determine the meaning of a word based on its use within the passage, which may differ from its everyday meaning.

Targeted Exercise:
Sample Sentence:
"Carla's approach to the new project was meticulous; she carefully examined every detail, aware that even a minor oversight could derail the entire operation."

Question: In this context, "meticulous" most nearly means:

- (A) disorganized

- (B) careless

- (C) thorough

- (D) hasty

Follow-Up Task: To reinforce vocabulary skills, rewrite the sentence using a synonym for "meticulous" that captures its meaning in this context (e.g., "thorough" or "detailed"). This exercise encourages flexibility with vocabulary and helps you recognize contextual meanings.

Simulating the SAT Reading Environment: Creating Realistic Practice Conditions

Simulating the testing environment is a powerful way to prepare for the SAT. Replicating real test conditions helps you build resilience to time constraints and stress, making the actual test feel familiar.

Steps to Create an SAT-Style Testing Environment

1. **Choose a Quiet, Dedicated Space**
   Find a place where you won't be interrupted. Ideally, practice in a space that resembles a testing environment: quiet, well-lit, and free from distractions.

2. **Stick to Strict Timing**
   Set a timer for each passage and adhere strictly to it. The goal is to develop a pacing instinct that will carry you through the real exam. As you practice, aim to complete each passage and its questions in 12-13 minutes.

3. **Replicate the Passage Sequence**
   On the SAT, passages are presented in a specific order (literature, social science, science, and historical documents). Practice passages in this order to grow accustomed to the flow, as shifting between genres tests different reading and analytical skills.

4. **Review Thoroughly After Each Practice Session**
   After completing a simulated test, spend ample time reviewing your answers. Note any trends in missed questions or areas where timing felt tight. This post-test reflection helps you understand your strengths and weaknesses, guiding future practice.

Full-Length Practice Exercise

For a complete simulation, select a reading passage set (e.g., five passages with 52 questions), set a timer for 65 minutes, and work through all questions consecutively. This full-length practice will challenge your endurance, pace, and accuracy. After completing the test, review each question, focusing on any mistakes and noting patterns in your responses.

Interactive Section: "Challenge for You" and Reflective Prompts

Challenge for You

Complete a timed reading passage (or full set) and answer these reflection questions afterward to assess your progress and deepen your understanding:

1. **How well did you manage your time for each question?**

2. **Which question type did you find most challenging?** Consider if it was inference, evidence-based, or vocabulary-in-context, and think about why.

3. **What strategies were most effective?** Were there specific techniques, like scanning or eliminating answer choices, that helped you succeed?

Reflective Prompts

1. **What specific steps helped improve your reading speed during this session?**

2. **Were there certain passage types (e.g., science, literature) that took longer?** Reflect on how you can adjust your approach to those sections.

3. **Which question types have you seen the most improvement in?** How can you build on this progress in future practice?

These prompts will keep you engaged in active learning, helping you track your development and adjust your strategies over time.

Inspiration Corner: Success Story

Success Story: Meet Liam. Initially, Liam found himself struggling with timing, often rushing through the final questions of each passage. To improve, he committed to full-length practice sessions once a week, simulating real SAT conditions. By analyzing each mistake post-test, he identified a pattern: inference questions often slowed him down. With extra focus on inference practice and regular timed drills, Liam eventually saw a steady improvement in both speed and accuracy, leading to a significant increase in his SAT Reading score.

Final Takeaway: Your Path to SAT Success

Practicing with purpose and using a structured approach will prepare you to navigate the SAT Reading section with confidence. Use these drills, targeted exercises, and test simulations to steadily build both your comprehension and test-taking skills. Every practice session brings you closer to mastery— embrace each challenge, track your progress, and remember that consistency is the key to success.

4.5 Improving Your Vocabulary for the SAT

Building a robust vocabulary is an essential part of mastering the SAT Reading section, and the benefits extend beyond the test itself. In this subsection, you'll find practical strategies for developing your vocabulary in a way that's both effective and sustainable, with a special focus on the most frequently tested words on the Digital SAT. From flashcards and contextual guessing techniques to daily practice methods, these strategies will empower you to approach vocabulary questions confidently, even when you encounter unfamiliar words.

Building a Strong SAT Vocabulary with Flashcards and Daily Practice

Expanding your vocabulary may seem daunting, but with consistent, manageable steps, it becomes an enjoyable and rewarding process. Daily practice is key to long-term retention, and flashcards are one of the most effective tools to facilitate this.

Creating and Using Flashcards Effectively

Why Flashcards? Flashcards offer a convenient way to study in short bursts, making it easy to integrate vocabulary practice into your daily routine. The key to success lies in making your flashcard practice interactive and engaging.

Step-by-Step Guide to Building Your Flashcards:

1. **Choose Relevant Words**: Focus on high-frequency SAT vocabulary words, especially those that appear frequently in past tests. These include words like *ambiguous, corroborate, mitigate*, and *nuance*, which often appear in both reading passages and questions.

2. **Create Detailed Flashcards**: For each word, include:

    o   **Definition**: Write a concise, easy-to-understand definition.

    o   **Synonyms and Antonyms**: Listing a few synonyms and antonyms helps you understand the word's nuances.

    o   **Example Sentence**: Include a sentence using the word in context, as this aids retention and understanding.

3. **Incorporate Visual Cues**: Studies show that associating words with images improves recall. Try drawing or adding small symbols on your flashcards (e.g., a checkmark for words with a positive meaning, an "X" for negative connotations).

Flashcard Practice Techniques:

-   **Spaced Repetition**: Review words at gradually increasing intervals. Start by reviewing daily, then every other day, and eventually weekly. This technique strengthens memory over time.

-   **The Five-Word Challenge**: Choose five new words each day and challenge yourself to use them in sentences or conversations. Regular usage helps solidify understanding.

Daily Practice Techniques to Strengthen Vocabulary

Consistent exposure and usage are essential for truly mastering vocabulary. Daily practice doesn't need to be time-consuming—it's all about integrating learning into your routine in ways that feel natural.

Methods for Daily Practice:

-   **Morning Word Routine**: Begin each morning by choosing a "word of the day." Write it down, review its definition, and use it at least once during the day, either in writing or conversation.

- **Weekly Vocabulary Themes**: Focus on a theme each week, such as emotions, argumentation, or nature, and select words that fit that theme. This strategy allows you to see how words relate to each other and understand their contextual nuances.

- **Digital Tools for Vocabulary Practice**: Use language apps like Quizlet, Anki, or the SAT-specific flashcard sets provided as a bonus with this book. These platforms offer customizable vocabulary decks and track your progress, providing reminders for spaced repetition practice.

Example: Imagine you're learning the word "pragmatic." Here's a flashcard you could create:

Word	**Pragmatic**
Definition	Dealing with problems realistically rather than ideally
Synonyms	Practical, sensible
Antonyms	Idealistic, impractical
Example	"His pragmatic approach to solving the issue impressed his colleagues."

By using this word in sentences, testing yourself on its synonyms, and reinforcing it through spaced repetition, you'll quickly gain a thorough understanding that will make it easier to recall during the test.

Contextual Guessing: How to Answer Vocabulary-in-Context Questions

Vocabulary-in-context questions on the SAT are less about memorization and more about interpreting meaning based on how a word is used within a passage. Developing skills in contextual guessing ensures that even when you encounter unfamiliar words, you can deduce their meaning effectively.

Strategy for Contextual Guessing

1. **Identify Surrounding Clues**: SAT passages often provide hints about a word's meaning in the sentences immediately surrounding it. Look for descriptive words, contrasting ideas, or examples that clarify the word.

2. **Consider the Word's Connotation**: Many SAT words have positive or negative connotations. Ask yourself if the word's tone matches a positive, negative, or neutral feeling, as this can help narrow down the answer choices.

3. **Apply the Process of Elimination**: SAT vocabulary questions often include answer choices with similar meanings. Use elimination to discard options that don't align with the sentence's context, leaving you with the most accurate choice.

Example of Contextual Guessing: *"After hearing about the sudden changes to the project, Clara felt apprehensive, a mix of worry and excitement bubbling inside her."*

Question: In this context, "apprehensive" most nearly means:

- (A) Thrilled

- (B) Confused

- (C) Anxious

- (D) Grateful

Breakdown:

- **Step 1: Identify Clues**: Words like "worry" and "excitement" imply that Clara's feelings are mixed but slightly leaning toward concern.

- **Step 2: Connotation Check**: Since "apprehensive" is not a positive word, choices like (A) Thrilled and (D) Grateful are less likely.

- **Step 3: Eliminate Choices**: Eliminate (A) and (D) based on tone, leaving (B) Confused and (C) Anxious. Given that "worry" aligns closely with "anxious," (C) is the best choice.

By practicing this step-by-step approach, you'll be better equipped to handle even the toughest vocabulary questions on the SAT.

How Expanding Your Vocabulary Enhances Overall Test Performance

A strong vocabulary does more than improve your score on vocabulary-specific questions—it enhances comprehension and interpretation across the entire test. Here's how vocabulary impacts each section:

1. **Improves Reading Comprehension**: In the reading section, a broader vocabulary allows you to grasp complex ideas, recognize subtle shifts in tone, and understand the author's intent more precisely. This translates to better performance on inference and evidence-based questions.

2. **Strengthens Analytical Skills for Writing**: The SAT Writing section often requires understanding the nuances of grammar and diction. A well-developed vocabulary aids in identifying the most accurate word choices and understanding contextual grammar rules.

3. **Boosts Confidence in Tackling Challenging Passages**: Familiarity with SAT-level vocabulary reduces the intimidation factor of challenging passages, allowing you to approach the text with confidence and focus on understanding rather than deciphering difficult words.

Case Study: Vocabulary in Action Consider Jenna, a student who struggled with SAT reading initially due to a limited vocabulary. She began using flashcards daily and practiced contextual guessing with passages. Over time, she noticed that not only did vocabulary questions feel easier, but she was also better able to understand complex arguments and author's tone in reading passages. This holistic improvement in her comprehension skills contributed to a significant score increase.

Interactive Section: Challenges and Reflection

Challenge for You
To solidify your understanding, here's a challenge to test your vocabulary skills.

1. **Flashcard Challenge**: Pick five new SAT words from a practice list and create detailed flashcards. Use each word in a sentence related to a current event or something in your life. Check back in a week to see if you can still recall the words without looking.

2. **Contextual Guessing Exercise**: Select a passage from an SAT prep book, choose one vocabulary question, and follow the contextual guessing steps outlined. Write down each step you took to reach your

answer and note any difficulties. This reflection can help you refine your guessing strategies.

Reflective Prompts:

1. **Which new vocabulary strategy has been the most helpful for you? Why?**

2. **Have you noticed an improvement in your reading comprehension as your vocabulary has expanded?**

3. **How do you plan to continue practicing vocabulary after you've built a foundation?**

Reflecting on these prompts after each practice session helps reinforce your vocabulary development and encourages consistent progress.

Motivation Corner: Success Story

Meet David: David was initially daunted by the SAT vocabulary. He started by setting aside 15 minutes each day to review flashcards, choosing five new words each week and practicing contextual guessing strategies with sample passages. Within a few months, he found that challenging passages became easier to understand, and his vocabulary-in-context question accuracy improved significantly. By test day, he felt prepared and confident, ultimately achieving a high score in the reading section.

Final Takeaway: Mastering Vocabulary for Lasting Success

Building a strong vocabulary is a journey that extends far beyond the SAT. With these techniques, you're not only preparing for test day but also developing skills that will enhance your reading, writing, and critical thinking abilities for years to come. Embrace each practice session, apply these strategies consistently, and watch as your vocabulary—and your confidence— grows with each passing day.

Chapter 5: Conquering the Writing and Language Section

5.1 Understanding the Writing and Language Section

The Writing and Language section of the Digital SAT is designed to assess your ability to identify and correct errors in grammar, punctuation, sentence structure, and writing style. Mastering this section not only boosts your overall SAT score but also strengthens your academic writing skills, essential for success in college. Here, we'll explore the structure of the Writing and Language section, focus on critical grammar and punctuation rules, examine common writing issues tested on the SAT, and provide interactive exercises to reinforce these concepts.

Structure of the Writing and Language Section

The Writing and Language section presents you with passages on diverse topics, from history and social sciences to humanities and science. Each passage includes a series of questions testing specific skills, divided into two main categories:

1. **Standard English Conventions**
   These questions focus on grammar, punctuation, and sentence

structure. They require a strong understanding of fundamental English rules, including:

- o **Subject-Verb Agreement**: Ensuring verbs match their subjects in number.

- o **Pronoun Clarity and Agreement**: Making sure pronouns refer clearly and match their antecedents.

- o **Verb Tense Consistency**: Ensuring all verbs are in the correct tense and consistent throughout the sentence.

- o **Parallel Structure**: Maintaining consistent structure, especially in lists and comparisons.

- o **Punctuation Usage**: Using commas, semicolons, and colons accurately.

2. **Expression of Ideas**
   These questions test your ability to enhance clarity, coherence, and precision in writing. You'll be asked to improve sentence structure, choose more accurate words, and reorganize information for better flow.

Each question type is designed to evaluate your ability to edit and improve written material, a skill vital not only for SAT success but also for academic writing.

Key Grammar, Punctuation, and Sentence Structure Rules for the SAT

Let's dive into the fundamental rules you'll need to master to excel in the Writing and Language section. These rules are some of the most frequently tested concepts on the SAT, so understanding them thoroughly will help you approach questions with confidence.

1. Subject-Verb Agreement

In subject-verb agreement questions, the subject and verb in a sentence must match in number (singular or plural). Errors in agreement often occur when other words or phrases are placed between the subject and verb, creating confusion.

Examples:

- **Correct**: "The team of scientists *is* working on a new project."

- **Incorrect**: "The team of scientists *are* working on a new project."

Practice Tip: To ensure agreement, isolate the subject and verb. Ignore intervening words or phrases that might confuse the sentence structure.

Exercise: Correct the subject-verb agreement in the following sentences.

1. "The group of musicians *are* setting up their instruments."

2. "Each of the athletes *were* excited for the competition."

3. "A collection of rare coins *have* been displayed in the museum."

2. Pronoun Clarity and Agreement

Pronouns should clearly refer to a specific noun (antecedent) and must agree in both number and gender. Vague or ambiguous pronouns create confusion and reduce clarity.

Examples:

- **Correct**: "The student forgot *his or her* notebook."

- **Incorrect**: "The student forgot *their* notebook." (when referring to a single student)

Practice Tip: Whenever you see a pronoun, check its antecedent. Ask yourself, "Is it clear who or what this pronoun refers to?"

Challenge for You: Rewrite the following sentences to ensure pronoun clarity.

1. "When Jamie met Alex, *he* was very nervous." (Who was nervous?)

2. "The dog ran to the owner because *they* called." (Who called the dog?)

3. Parallel Structure

Parallel structure, or parallelism, means that items in a series or list should have the same grammatical form. This rule is especially important in comparisons and lists.

Examples:

- **Correct**: "She enjoys reading, writing, and jogging."

- **Incorrect**: "She enjoys reading, writing, and to jog."

Practice Tip: Break down lists or comparisons into individual parts. If one part doesn't match the structure of the others, you may have a parallelism issue.

Exercise: Identify and correct errors in parallel structure.

1. "In his free time, Jacob likes painting, to cook, and going for hikes."

2. "The company values hard work, commitment, and people who are creative."

4. Verb Tense Consistency

Verb tense consistency is essential for clear, logical sentences. Ensure that verbs remain in the same tense unless there is a reason to change them (e.g., shifting from past to present for a different time frame).

Examples:

- **Correct**: "She studied all night and *earned* high marks."

- **Incorrect**: "She studied all night and *earns* high marks."

Practice Tip: Identify time cues in the sentence (e.g., "yesterday" or "will") to determine the correct verb tense.

Exercise: Correct the verb tense errors.

1. "After the meeting *ended*, everyone *goes* to lunch."

2. "She *was writing* the report when her boss *calls* her."

Common Punctuation Rules

Accurate punctuation is essential for clarity and sentence flow. Below are the most critical punctuation rules to focus on:

1. Commas in Compound Sentences

In compound sentences, place a comma before a coordinating conjunction (for, and, nor, but, or, yet, so) that joins two independent clauses.

Examples:

- **Correct**: "He wanted to join the team, *but* he didn't meet the requirements."

- **Incorrect**: "He wanted to join the team but he didn't meet the requirements."

2. Apostrophes for Possession and Contractions

Use apostrophes to show possession or form contractions. Avoid using apostrophes to make nouns plural.

Examples:

- **Possession**: "The teacher's notes were thorough."

- **Contraction**: "It's going to rain." ("It's" = It is)

3. Semicolons for Related Independent Clauses

A semicolon links two independent clauses that are closely related without using a conjunction.

Examples:

- **Correct**: "She enjoys traveling; her favorite place is Italy."

- **Incorrect**: "She enjoys traveling, her favorite place is Italy."

Challenge for You: Insert correct punctuation in the following sentences.

1. "The project was difficult yet rewarding."

2. "It is Jims book not Sarahs."

3. "She studied hard she aced the test."

Identifying Common Writing Issues in SAT Questions

Beyond grammar and punctuation, the SAT Writing and Language section often tests specific writing issues, such as misplaced modifiers, wordiness, and shifts in tone. Understanding these will help you quickly spot and fix errors.

1. Misplaced Modifiers

Modifiers must be placed near the word or phrase they modify. Misplaced modifiers can make sentences confusing or awkward.

Examples:

- **Correct**: "Exhausted, the runner collapsed at the finish line."

- **Incorrect**: "The runner collapsed, exhausted, at the finish line."

Practice Tip: To check for misplaced modifiers, locate the modifier and ask, "What does this word or phrase modify?" If it's unclear, rewrite the sentence.

2. Wordiness and Redundancy

The SAT values conciseness. Avoid redundant phrases and unnecessary words, which can clutter sentences and make them less effective.

Examples:

- **Correct**: "She joined the meeting promptly."

- **Incorrect**: "She joined the meeting at the time of its beginning promptly."

Challenge for You: Rewrite the following sentence to remove redundancy.

- "He returned back to his hometown."

3. Shifts in Tone and Style

Consistency in tone is crucial for clear communication. Shifts in tone, particularly from formal to informal language, are commonly tested on the SAT.

Examples:

- **Correct**: "The report outlines significant trends in the economy."

- **Incorrect**: "The report outlines some pretty awesome trends in the economy."

Interactive Section: Practice and Self-Reflection

Challenge for You
Here are sentences with errors for you to correct. Identify and correct issues with grammar, punctuation, and sentence structure.

1. "The group of dancers, who was extremely talented, performed their routine flawlessly."

2. "After the meeting ended everyone goes to lunch."

3. "Each of the team members are bringing their own supplies."

Reflection Questions:

1. Which types of errors were easiest to spot? Which were more challenging?

2. Did you find any patterns in your approach to finding and fixing errors?

3. How might you improve your editing strategy for better results on the SAT?

Key Takeaways

1. **Grammar and Punctuation Rules**: Focus on subject-verb agreement, pronoun clarity, parallel structure, and punctuation for accurate answers.

2. **Common Writing Issues**: Avoid misplaced modifiers, redundancy, and shifts in tone to improve clarity.

3. **Consistent Practice**: Regularly practice identifying and correcting these errors to build accuracy and confidence.

Final Advice: As you study for the SAT Writing and Language section, remember that each question is an opportunity to refine your editing skills. Practice these concepts thoroughly, use the exercises to reinforce your understanding, and approach each passage as if you're a writer enhancing clarity and precision. With a clear understanding of these rules and regular practice, you'll develop a strong foundation for achieving a high score on the SAT Writing section.

5.2 Grammar Rules You Must Know

This subchapter is your comprehensive guide to the essential grammar rules tested on the Digital SAT's Writing and Language section. We'll break down each rule in detail, include practical examples, and offer interactive exercises so you can practice applying these concepts confidently. The goal is for you to understand not just how to spot errors, but also why these rules improve clarity and accuracy in writing.

Essential Grammar Rules for the SAT: Detailed Breakdown

Let's dive into three key areas of grammar frequently tested on the SAT: **subject-verb agreement, parallelism**, and **pronoun usage**. These areas are foundational, and mastering them will improve your ability to approach SAT questions efficiently and accurately.

---

1. Subject-Verb Agreement

Subject-verb agreement ensures that singular subjects are matched with singular verbs, and plural subjects with plural verbs. While this might sound straightforward, errors can easily slip in when additional phrases or clauses interrupt the main subject-verb relationship.

Detailed Explanation and Examples:

- **Basic Agreement**: The subject and verb in a sentence must agree in number.

    o **Correct**: "The *team is* practicing for the tournament."

    o **Incorrect**: "The *team are* practicing for the tournament." (Here, "team" is singular, so it should be "is.")

- **Interrupting Phrases**: When phrases like "along with," "in addition to," or "as well as" come between the subject and verb, ignore these phrases to determine the subject-verb agreement.

    o **Correct**: "The *teacher*, along with her students, *is* planning the event."

    o **Incorrect**: "The *teacher*, along with her students, *are* planning the event."

- **Subjects Joined by "Or" or "Nor"**: When subjects are connected by "or" or "nor," the verb should agree with the subject closest to it.

    o **Correct**: "Neither the manager *nor the employees are* available."

    o **Incorrect**: "Neither the manager *nor the employees is* available."

Practice Exercise: Correct the subject-verb agreement in these sentences.

1. "The collection of artifacts *are* being displayed at the museum."

2. "Either the captain or the players *is* responsible for the equipment."

3. "The bouquet of roses *were* placed on the table."

---

2. Parallelism

Parallelism, or parallel structure, means that elements in a list or comparison should have the same grammatical form. This rule is especially relevant for sentences containing lists, paired elements, or comparisons, as it ensures clarity and balance.

In-Depth Explanation and Examples:

- **Lists**: Each item in a list should match in form, usually in tense or part of speech.

    o **Correct**: "The proposal suggests revising policies, increasing funding, and hiring additional staff."

    o **Incorrect**: "The proposal suggests revising policies, to increase funding, and hiring additional staff." (Here, "to increase funding" disrupts the parallel structure.)

- **Correlative Conjunctions**: When using pairs like "either/or," "neither/nor," "not only/but also," ensure that the elements on each side match.

    o **Correct**: "She is not only intelligent *but also* hardworking."

    o **Incorrect**: "She is not only intelligent *but also works hard*." (Inconsistent structure)

Practice Tip: For sentences with lists or comparisons, isolate each item and read it separately to ensure it matches the others.

Challenge for You: Rewrite these sentences to correct any errors in parallel structure.

1. "In his free time, Jack enjoys reading novels, to play the guitar, and hiking in the mountains."

2. "The new policy will affect teachers, administrators, and how students are graded."

---

3. Pronoun Usage and Clarity

Pronouns should always clearly refer to a specific noun (antecedent) and must agree with that noun in both number and gender. Unclear pronoun references create ambiguity and can lead to misunderstandings in writing.

Detailed Explanation and Examples:

- **Clear Antecedent**: Every pronoun should clearly refer to one specific noun. Avoid using a pronoun if there is any ambiguity about what it refers to.

  - **Correct**: "When *Sarah* met *Amanda, she* introduced herself."

  - **Incorrect**: "When *Sarah* met *Amanda, she* was excited." (It's unclear who was excited.)

- **Agreement in Number and Gender**: Pronouns should match their antecedents in number (singular/plural) and gender.

  - **Correct**: "Each student should complete *his or her* assignment."

  - **Incorrect**: "Each student should complete *their* assignment." (In formal writing, avoid using "their" for singular nouns.)

Interactive Exercise: Improve pronoun clarity in these sentences.

1. "When Maria talked to James, *he* shared the news." (Who shared the news?)

2. "The dogs chased the ball because *it* was thrown." (Clarify what "it" refers to.)

Punctuation Rules: Commas, Semicolons, and Colons

Mastering punctuation is key to clear and coherent writing. The SAT frequently tests your understanding of commas, semicolons, and colons, especially in complex sentences.

---

1. Commas in Compound and Complex Sentences

Commas are essential for separating elements and clarifying meaning. In compound sentences, commas should precede coordinating conjunctions (for, and, nor, but, or, yet, so) that link two independent clauses.

Explanation and Examples:

- **Compound Sentences**: A comma should precede the conjunction linking two independent clauses.

  o **Correct**: "He studied diligently, *and* he achieved high scores."

  o **Incorrect**: "He studied diligently and he achieved high scores."

- **Introductory Phrases and Nonessential Information**: Use commas to separate introductory elements or nonessential clauses.

  o **Correct**: "After the meeting, the team discussed their next steps."

  o **Incorrect**: "After the meeting the team discussed their next steps."

Exercise: Insert commas where needed in the following sentences.

1. "Because she practiced regularly she improved her skills significantly."

2. "The painting which was created by a famous artist sold for a high price."

---

2. Semicolons to Link Related Independent Clauses

A semicolon can join two independent clauses that are closely related, especially when you want to avoid a conjunction.

Examples:

- **Correct**: "The storm was approaching; the residents prepared to evacuate."

- **Incorrect**: "The storm was approaching, the residents prepared to evacuate." (This is a comma splice.)

Practice Tip: To test if a semicolon is appropriate, replace it with a period. If both parts stand alone as sentences, a semicolon is likely correct.

Challenge: Correct the punctuation in these sentences using semicolons.

1. "The results were surprising everyone had expected a different outcome."

2. "He didn't enjoy the book it was too long and complex."

3. Colons to Introduce Lists or Explanations

A colon is used after an independent clause to introduce a list, a quotation, or further explanation.

Examples:

- **Correct**: "She needs to buy several items: bread, milk, and eggs."

- **Incorrect**: "She needs to buy: bread, milk, and eggs." (The colon should follow an independent clause.)

Practice Exercise: Determine if the colons are used correctly in these sentences.

1. "His hobbies include: hiking, biking, and swimming."

2. "The committee reached a consensus: the project would go forward."

Correcting Run-Ons and Sentence Fragments

Errors in sentence structure, such as run-ons and fragments, disrupt clarity and readability. Here's how to recognize and fix them.

1. Run-On Sentences

A run-on sentence occurs when two or more independent clauses are joined without proper punctuation or conjunctions. Run-ons can be corrected by separating clauses with a period, semicolon, or coordinating conjunction.

Examples:

- **Incorrect**: "She was late to the meeting it was hard to find parking."

- **Correction**: "She was late to the meeting *because* it was hard to find parking."

Practice: Rewrite these run-on sentences to improve clarity.

1. "The movie was long I didn't enjoy it."

2. "She tried to finish her work it was already late."

2. Sentence Fragments

A sentence fragment is an incomplete sentence, often missing a subject, verb, or complete thought. Fragments lack the information needed to stand alone as sentences.

Examples:

- **Incorrect**: "Although he wanted to join."

- **Correction**: "Although he wanted to join, he had other commitments."

Challenge for You: Rewrite these fragments to create complete sentences.

1. "Running through the park on a beautiful day."

2. "Because she studied hard."

Interactive Practice: Grammar Challenges

Here's a set of sentences with common grammar, punctuation, and structure errors. Correct each one, and review the changes you made.

1. "The orchestra members *was* tuning their instruments."

2. "Neither John nor Sarah *are* ready to present."

3. "He likes to play basketball, going hiking, and to swim."

4. "I wanted to go on vacation but I had too much work."

5. "The results were surprising everyone was shocked."

Key Takeaways and Tips

1. **Subject-Verb Agreement**: Ensure subjects and verbs agree, ignoring interrupting phrases.

2. **Parallelism**: Keep lists and comparisons grammatically consistent.

3. **Pronoun Usage**: Use pronouns with clear antecedents and ensure they match in number and gender.

4. **Punctuation**: Remember to use commas in compound sentences, semicolons to link independent clauses, and colons for lists or explanations.

5. **Avoid Run-Ons and Fragments**: Ensure each sentence is complete and correctly structured.

By thoroughly understanding these grammar rules and practicing consistently, you'll be able to recognize and correct errors with greater accuracy. The exercises and examples provided will prepare you to tackle the SAT Writing and Language section confidently, and these grammar skills will enhance your writing for academic and professional success.

5.3 Improving Sentence and Paragraph Structure

In the Writing and Language section of the Digital SAT, mastering the organization and structure of sentences and paragraphs is crucial for crafting clear and logical writing. This subchapter will guide you through essential techniques to improve paragraph flow, integrate effective transition words, and remove redundancy and wordiness in sentences. By applying these methods, you'll learn to create responses that are coherent, concise, and polished.

Enhancing Paragraph Flow by Rearranging Sentences

Improving the flow of a paragraph often involves rearranging sentences so that ideas progress logically. A well-structured paragraph helps readers understand the main point and follow supporting details without confusion. Here's a step-by-step approach to achieving effective paragraph flow.

Steps for Rearranging Sentences to Improve Paragraph Flow

1. **Identify the Topic Sentence and Main Idea**
   The topic sentence typically introduces the main idea of the paragraph. Starting with this sentence provides a foundation for readers to understand the paragraph's purpose. Once you have the main idea clear, arrange supporting sentences to build on or clarify it.

   o **Example:**

     ▪ *Disordered*:

        ▪ "Furthermore, volunteering provides social benefits."

        ▪ "It can also improve mental health by providing a sense of purpose."

        ▪ "Volunteering offers valuable help to communities."

     ▪ *Revised (Ordered)*:

        ▪ "Volunteering offers valuable help to communities."

        ▪ "It can also improve mental health by providing a sense of purpose."

        ▪ "Furthermore, volunteering provides social benefits."

2. **Use Supporting Details in a Logical Order**
   Think about how the information flows: Does it follow a cause-and-effect pattern, a chronological sequence, or a general-to-specific order? Choose a logical sequence that best fits the information presented in the paragraph.

   o **Example:** If describing the process of photosynthesis, a chronological or step-by-step order makes the most sense. If contrasting two viewpoints, a "point-counterpoint" order might be more effective.

3. **Check for Smooth Transitions Between Ideas**
   Each sentence should logically lead to the next. Use transition words or phrases to signal connections between ideas, especially if the sentences convey different types of information (e.g., cause and effect, contrast, examples).

- o **Example:**

  - *Without Transitions*: "Exercise improves cardiovascular health. It also boosts mood. It can be challenging to find time for exercise."

  - *With Transitions*: "Exercise improves cardiovascular health. *Moreover*, it boosts mood. *However*, it can be challenging to find time for exercise."

Using Transition Words for Cohesion Between Ideas

Transition words play a significant role in connecting ideas, helping readers understand relationships between sentences. Effective transitions can indicate addition, contrast, cause and effect, or conclusion, ensuring a cohesive and understandable paragraph.

Types of Transition Words and How to Use Them

1. **Transitions for Adding Information**
   Use these transitions to add similar points or continue an idea.

   - o **Examples:** "Additionally," "Furthermore," "In addition"

   - o **Example in Use**: "Regular exercise has physical health benefits. *Additionally*, it helps improve mental well-being."

2. **Transitions for Contrast or Opposing Ideas**
   These transitions signal a shift to an opposing or different idea.

   - o **Examples:** "However," "Conversely," "On the other hand"

   - o **Example in Use**: "Technology has connected people globally. *However*, it has also led to increased isolation in some cases."

3. **Transitions for Cause and Effect**
   These indicate a causal relationship between ideas.

   - o **Examples:** "Therefore," "As a result," "Consequently"

   - o **Example in Use**: "She studied diligently for weeks. *As a result*, she achieved a high score on the test."

4. **Transitions for Emphasis or Examples**
   Use these to highlight a point or introduce specific examples.

   - o **Examples**: "For instance," "In particular," "Specifically"

   - o **Example in Use**: "Reading offers many benefits. *For instance*, it can improve vocabulary and comprehension skills."

Practice Tips for Using Transitions

- **Vary Your Transitions**: Avoid overusing the same transitions. Instead, select the most fitting word for the relationship you want to convey.

- **Test Your Transitions**: Read sentences without the transition. Then, add a transition and read it again to see if it enhances clarity or flow.

- **Maintain a Natural Flow**: Transitions should feel organic. Avoid forcing transitions where none are needed, as this can make the writing feel choppy or overly formal.

Challenge for You: Insert appropriate transitions into these sentences to improve flow.

1. "The company implemented new policies to improve productivity. _____, employee satisfaction increased."

2. "Many people enjoy traveling. _____, some find it tiring and stressful."

Fixing Redundancy and Wordiness in Sentence Structure

Concise writing eliminates unnecessary words and redundant phrases, resulting in clear, impactful sentences. In the SAT Writing section, mastering conciseness helps you avoid repetitive language and focus on the main point.

Identifying and Eliminating Redundant Phrases

Redundancy occurs when a sentence includes words or phrases that repeat the same idea, leading to unnecessary length without adding meaning.

Examples of Common Redundant Phrases:

- "Advance planning" → "Planning"

- "Close proximity" → "Proximity"

- "Free gift" → "Gift"

Examples in Context:

- **Incorrect:** "In my personal opinion, the event was a success."

- **Correct:** "In my opinion, the event was a success."

- **Incorrect:** "He returned back to his hometown."

- **Correct:** "He returned to his hometown."

Practice Exercise: Rewrite the following sentences to remove redundancy.

1. "The final outcome of the experiment was unexpected and surprising."

2. "Each and every member contributed to the project."

Reducing Wordiness for Conciseness

Wordiness occurs when sentences contain extra words or overly complex phrases that obscure the main idea. Reducing wordiness makes sentences more direct and engaging.

Examples of Wordiness:

- **Incorrect:** "At this point in time, we are unable to make a decision."

- **Correct:** "We cannot make a decision now."

- **Incorrect:** "Due to the fact that she practiced daily, she improved."

- **Correct:** "Because she practiced daily, she improved."

Tips for Reducing Wordiness:

- Replace long phrases with simpler words.

- Use active voice instead of passive voice where possible.

- Focus on the main point, avoiding unnecessary details that do not add to the core message.

Challenge for You: Rewrite these sentences to make them more concise.

1. "She completed the assignment in a very efficient manner."

2. "The reason why he left was due to the fact that he felt unappreciated."

Applying Techniques: Improving a Paragraph Step-by-Step

Now that you understand the basics of improving paragraph structure, let's apply these techniques to an entire paragraph. By following each step, we'll transform a disorganized, wordy paragraph into a clear and logical one.

Original Paragraph:

"Studying regularly is important for academic success. It allows students to retain information better. Regular study habits also reduce stress before exams. Some students study in groups, which helps them understand difficult topics better. Studying alone, on the other hand, allows for more focus on personal weaknesses."

Step 1: Identify and Order Key Ideas

To create flow, start by organizing the paragraph around the main point, supporting ideas, and contrasting points.

1. **Main Idea**: Studying regularly is essential.

2. **Supporting Ideas**: Benefits of studying regularly, such as information retention and stress reduction.

3. **Contrasting Point**: Differences between group study and solo study.

Step 2: Use Transitions to Link Ideas

Use transitions to connect benefits of studying and clarify the contrast between studying in groups vs. alone.

- *Revised*: "Studying regularly is essential for academic success because it allows students to retain information and reduces stress before exams. *Additionally*, group study can help students understand difficult topics, *while* studying alone allows them to focus on personal weaknesses."

Step 3: Eliminate Redundancy and Wordiness

Look for unnecessary repetition, and reduce wordy phrases to enhance clarity.

- *Further Revised*: "Studying regularly is essential for academic success as it helps students retain information and reduces pre-exam stress.

Moreover, group study can aid in understanding complex topics, *whereas* solo study allows students to address personal challenges."

Final Version:
"Studying regularly is essential for academic success as it helps students retain information and reduces pre-exam stress. Moreover, group study can aid in understanding complex topics, whereas solo study allows students to address personal challenges."

Practice Challenge: Try applying the same process to the paragraph below.

- "Learning a new skill can be difficult at first. People who stick with it eventually see improvement. Having a regular practice schedule helps. Additionally, learning with friends makes it more enjoyable. Practicing alone, on the other hand, allows more focus on individual progress."

Key Points to Remember

1. **Rearrange Sentences for Logical Flow**: Start with a main idea, arrange supporting details logically, and use transitions to create a coherent structure.

2. **Use Transition Words Thoughtfully**: Choose transition words that clarify the relationship between ideas, making the text easier to follow.

3. **Eliminate Redundancy and Wordiness**: Focus on concise language by removing repeated ideas and simplifying phrases, ensuring each word adds value to the sentence.

By practicing these techniques, you'll be able to enhance clarity, improve readability, and strengthen coherence in your writing. This skill set is invaluable not only for the SAT but also for effective communication in academic and professional settings. Consistent practice and application of these principles will help you tackle SAT Writing questions confidently, leading to a higher score and a clearer writing style.

5.4 Practice Drills for Writing and Language

In this subchapter, we'll dive deep into targeted practice exercises designed to help you master each type of question in the Writing and Language section of the Digital SAT. Through a mix of editing techniques, grammar-focused drills, and timed practice, you'll build the accuracy and speed necessary to excel in this section. Each exercise is accompanied by detailed explanations, enabling you to reinforce grammar knowledge, sharpen editing skills, and approach the SAT with confidence.

How to Approach Editing Questions with Efficiency

Developing an efficient approach to editing questions is essential for performing well under the SAT's time constraints. Editing questions are designed to test your ability to spot and correct errors swiftly. Here's a step-by-step guide to help you navigate these questions with accuracy.

Step 1: Read the Entire Sentence Carefully

Before jumping to conclusions about potential errors, read the entire sentence. Often, a quick scan can highlight obvious errors in grammar, structure, or punctuation, but taking a moment to absorb the sentence as a whole helps you catch more subtle issues.

- **Example:**
    - Original: "Each student *must* complete their assignments on time."
    - First Observation: The pronoun "their" doesn't agree with "Each student" (singular).
    - **Correction:** "Each student must complete *his or her* assignments on time."

Step 2: Identify the Type of Error

Once you've read the sentence, determine the nature of the potential error. Common SAT question types include errors in **subject-verb agreement**, **pronoun usage**, **parallel structure**, and **punctuation**. Identifying the specific rule at play will guide your choice of answer.

- **Example:**
    - Original: "The scientist, as well as the students, *are* excited about the results."

- o **Error Type**: Subject-verb agreement (collective nouns).

- o **Correction**: "The scientist, as well as the students, *is* excited about the results."

Step 3: Use the Process of Elimination

Read through each answer choice, eliminating those that do not correct the identified error or introduce new errors. Choose the option that maintains clarity, grammatical accuracy, and appropriate tone.

- **Practice Tip**: Test each option by reading it aloud. Often, hearing the sentence can reveal issues in tone, structure, or flow.

Practice Exercise: Correct the following sentences by identifying errors and using the best answer choice.

1. "Everyone in the class were assigned *their* own projects."

   - o (A) was, their

   - o (B) were, his or her

   - o (C) was, his or her

   - o (D) were, they

   - o **Correct Answer**: (C) was, his or her

2. "The books on the shelf, along with the magazines, *need* to be organized."

   - o (A) need

   - o (B) needs

   - o **Correct Answer**: (B) needs

Practice Sets with Step-by-Step Explanations for Each Grammar Rule

The following practice sets focus on specific grammar rules commonly tested on the SAT. Each set includes explanations for every answer choice to strengthen your understanding of each rule.

Set 1: Subject-Verb Agreement

Question:

1. "The team of researchers *are* presenting their findings tomorrow."

   o (A) are

   o (B) is

   o (C) have been

   o (D) has been

Answer and Explanation:

   o **Correct Answer:** (B) *is*

   o **Explanation:** "Team" is a collective noun treated as singular in American English, so "team *is* presenting" is correct.

Set 2: Pronoun Clarity and Agreement

Question:
2. "If a person wants to succeed, *they* must work hard."

- (A) they

- (B) he or she

- (C) him or her

- (D) one

Answer and Explanation:

- **Correct Answer:** (B) *he or she*

- **Explanation:** "A person" is singular, so it requires a singular pronoun, making "he or she" the correct answer.

Set 3: Parallel Structure

Question:
3. "The project requires skills in communication, time management, and *to write reports*."

- (A) to write reports

- (B) writing reports

- (C) report writing

- (D) and reports

Answer and Explanation:

- **Correct Answer:** (B) *writing reports*

- **Explanation:** The sentence lists "skills in" areas, so maintaining a parallel structure with gerunds (communication, time management, and writing) is correct.

Interactive Challenge:

Rewrite the following sentence to correct any errors in structure or clarity.

- "The company values creativity, dedication, and people who are honest."

    o **Corrected Sentence:** "The company values creativity, dedication, and honesty."

Using Real SAT Writing Prompts for Timed Practice

Timed practice with real SAT prompts is a powerful way to simulate the actual test environment and improve your response speed. Set a timer for each exercise to get used to working within a specific time frame.

Prompt Exercise: Review the following paragraph and correct errors based on the rules we've covered.

Sample Prompt:
"Reading regularly can greatly improve vocabulary. Studies show that students who read daily *are developing* stronger analytical skills than those who don't. Furthermore, reading provides exposure to various writing styles, *which it allows* students to improve their own writing techniques. A love for reading, *also it* increases empathy and broadens perspectives."

Answers and Explanations:

1. **Error:** "*are developing* stronger analytical skills…"

    o **Correction:** "*develop* stronger analytical skills…"

    o **Explanation:** The present simple tense ("develop") is appropriate for a general statement about students.

2. **Error:** "which it allows…"

- o **Correction**: "which allows…"

- o **Explanation**: The pronoun "it" is unnecessary and creates redundancy.

3. **Error**: "A love for reading, *also it* increases…"

  - o **Correction**: "A love for reading also increases…"

  - o **Explanation**: The pronoun "it" is redundant and should be removed to streamline the sentence.

Tips for Timed Practice:

- **Set a 5-10 Minute Timer**: Complete the prompt within this timeframe to simulate the test experience.

- **Review and Reflect**: After the timer ends, go back and review each correction to understand why it was needed.

Interactive Exercises: "Challenge Yourself" Section

The "Challenge Yourself" section provides exercises to practice common SAT question types in the Writing and Language section. These questions cover a variety of grammatical rules and structural improvements.

Challenge Exercise: For each sentence below, identify and correct errors to improve clarity, structure, and grammar.

1. "Each of the team members *are* responsible for completing *their* tasks."

2. "During the workshop, Maria *talked about her projects* and also *she discussed* her goals for the future."

3. "It is important *to communicate clearly, writing effectively,* and *express yourself confidently*."

Answers and Explanations:

1. **Correction**: "Each of the team members *is* responsible for completing *his or her* tasks."

   - o **Explanation**: "Each" is a singular subject requiring "is," and "their" is corrected to "his or her" for pronoun agreement.

2. **Correction**: "During the workshop, Maria *talked about her projects and discussed her goals for the future.*"

   o **Explanation**: Removing "and also" creates a more concise sentence, while simplifying "she discussed" to "discussed" improves flow.

3. **Correction**: "It is important *to communicate clearly, write effectively,* and *express yourself confidently.*"

   o **Explanation**: Maintaining parallel structure in the list (communicate, write, express) makes the sentence consistent and clear.

Reflective Questions:

1. Were there any questions where you initially missed the error? What was challenging about these?

2. How can you adjust your approach to catch these types of errors more easily?

Key Takeaways and Study Tips

1. **Develop a Systematic Editing Approach**: Start with a full read-through of each sentence, identify potential errors, and use the process of elimination to choose the best answer.

2. **Master Core Grammar Rules**: Focus on rules frequently tested in the SAT, such as subject-verb agreement, pronoun usage, parallel structure, and punctuation.

3. **Practice with Real SAT Prompts Under Timed Conditions**: Set aside time to complete full prompts within time constraints to build your response speed and accuracy.

4. **Review and Reflect Regularly**: Consistently analyze your mistakes, ensuring you understand why each correction is necessary to improve accuracy in future exercises.

By diligently practicing these exercises and following a structured approach, you'll build the skills necessary to handle any Writing and Language question confidently on the Digital SAT. Remember, each practice session is a step toward mastering essential grammar rules, improving editing techniques, and enhancing your overall writing clarity. Keep practicing and reflecting on your progress, and approach each new challenge with confidence!

5.5 Writing with Precision Under Pressure

Performing well under time constraints requires a blend of quick analysis, strategic elimination of incorrect answers, and efficient use of time to allow for review. This subchapter provides in-depth strategies to help you approach each question with clarity, identify errors swiftly, and manage time effectively. By mastering these techniques, you'll be equipped to tackle the SAT Writing section with confidence and precision.

Quickly Analyzing Questions and Eliminating Incorrect Answers

The first step to success in the Writing and Language section is learning to quickly understand what each question asks. Many questions focus on clarity, grammar, or structure, so recognizing the type of correction required can save you valuable time.

Step-by-Step Guide to Efficient Question Analysis

1. **Determine the Primary Focus of the Question**
   Start by identifying the main error type. Look for signs that the question involves **grammar** (e.g., subject-verb agreement, pronoun clarity), **structure** (e.g., parallelism), or **style** (e.g., wordiness or redundancy). Recognizing the focus helps you zero in on the relevant parts of the sentence and ignore distractions.

   o **Example:** "Every participant should bring *their* own materials."

   ▪ **Error Focus:** Pronoun Agreement (the pronoun "their" doesn't match "Every participant," which is singular).

   ▪ **Correction:** "Every participant should bring *his or her* own materials."

2. **Preview the Answer Choices**
   Skim through the answer choices briefly to understand the types of

changes offered. This preview can highlight whether the question involves issues with **verb tense, subject-verb agreement,** or **conciseness**.

- o **Example Choices:**
  - ▪ (A) their
  - ▪ (B) his or her
  - ▪ (C) his and her
  - ▪ (D) each student's
- o **Quick Elimination**: Eliminate (A) due to pronoun mismatch, and (C) and (D) for awkward or unclear phrasing.

3. **Use Strategic Elimination**
   Systematically eliminate options that introduce new errors or do not align with the sentence's grammatical needs. This narrows down choices, improving your accuracy under time constraints.

4. **Choose the Most Concise Option**
   The SAT Writing section often rewards answers that are both grammatically correct and concise. Choose the answer that improves clarity without adding unnecessary words.

Practice Exercise: Analyze and Select the Correct Answer

For each sentence below, identify the main focus and choose the best answer based on your analysis.

1. "The team of engineers *are* presenting their design proposals next week."

   - o (A) are
   - o (B) is
   - o (C) will
   - o (D) were
   - o **Correct Answer**: (B) is
     - ▪ **Explanation**: "The team" is a collective noun treated as singular in American English, so "is" is correct.

146

2. "Her family decided to sell *their home, which they had lived in it* for over 20 years."

- o (A) their home, which they had lived in it

- o (B) their home, in which they had lived

- o (C) the home, in which they have been living it

- o (D) their home, which they have been living

- o **Correct Answer**: (B) their home, in which they had lived

   - ▪ **Explanation**: Answer (B) eliminates redundancy by removing "it" and correctly uses "in which" for clarity.

Using Time Wisely in the Writing Section to Review Answers

Effective time management can be the difference between answering all questions and leaving some unanswered. By developing a structured time-management approach, you'll have enough time for initial answers and a quick review.

Time-Management Techniques for Success

1. **Divide Time by Passage**
   Allocate a fixed amount of time per passage (e.g., around 7-8 minutes if you have four passages to complete in 35 minutes). Keeping to a set time for each passage ensures that you won't linger too long on any one section, giving you a balanced approach.

2. **Flag Questions for Review**
   If a question feels ambiguous or takes too long, mark it for review. This allows you to maintain your pace without getting bogged down by challenging questions.

3. **Save a Few Minutes for Final Review**
   Aim to finish each passage slightly ahead of schedule, leaving a few minutes for a final review. Use this time to revisit flagged questions and recheck commonly tested areas, such as subject-verb agreement and parallel structure.

4. **Double-Check Key Grammar and Structure Rules**
   During review, quickly check for high-frequency errors like pronoun

clarity, verb tense consistency, and punctuation. Even a brief review can help you catch easy-to-miss errors, improving your accuracy.

Reflective Practice: Time Your Progress

After each practice session, assess your time allocation:

1. Did you complete each passage within the target time?

2. Which question types took the longest, and how can you improve your speed?

3. Did you leave enough time for review, and were you able to improve flagged answers?

Practicing Strategies for Balancing Speed and Accuracy

Achieving a balance between speed and accuracy requires strategic practice. The following exercises and techniques help you build efficiency while maintaining focus on accuracy.

Exercises for Building Speed and Accuracy

1. **Timed Practice with Gradual Speed Increase**
   Begin your practice with a relaxed time limit (e.g., 10 minutes per passage). Over time, gradually reduce this limit by 30-60 seconds to build your response speed. This method trains you to process information faster without compromising accuracy.

2. **Focus Drills for High-Impact Question Types**
   If certain question types slow you down, dedicate extra practice to them. For example, if transitions or parallel structure questions take longer, focus on these until they become quicker to recognize and address.

3. **The "Two-Reads" Technique**
   For sentences with complex phrasing or multiple errors, use a two-read approach: the first read for identifying structural or grammatical issues and the second for clarity and style. This technique helps ensure you don't overlook any subtle errors.

4. **Skip-and-Return Method**
   Use this method to quickly answer questions you feel confident

about, then circle back to tougher ones. This strategy prevents you from losing time and helps keep your momentum steady.

Sample Timed Drill

Set a 5-minute timer and attempt the following question, focusing on accuracy while being aware of time.

Sample Question:
"The company's new policy *seeks to reduce* office waste but also *to encourage* employees to recycle."

- (A) seeks to reduce, to encourage

- (B) seeks to reduce, encourages

- (C) is seeking to reduce, encourages

- (D) reduces, encourages

Answer and Explanation:

- **Correct Answer**: (A) seeks to reduce, to encourage

- **Explanation**: Option (A) maintains parallel structure, keeping both verbs in the same infinitive form.

Interactive Section: "Challenge Yourself" Practice

These "Challenge Yourself" exercises are designed to reinforce your skills in identifying and correcting common SAT Writing errors under time constraints.

Challenge Exercise 1: Identify and Correct Errors
Each sentence has a grammatical or structural error. Under a 1-minute time limit per question, identify and correct the issues.

1. "The students and teachers *is* preparing for the annual festival, which *they has* been planning for months."

2. "She enjoyed not only traveling to new places, *but also to try* new foods."

3. "The results of the survey, *which it was conducted last year,* were released yesterday."

Answers and Explanations:

1. **Correction:** "The students and teachers *are* preparing for the annual festival, which *they have* been planning for months."

    o   **Explanation:** Correct subject-verb agreement with "students and teachers" (plural) requires "are," and "they have" correctly matches the present perfect tense.

2. **Correction:** "She enjoyed not only traveling to new places, *but also trying* new foods."

    o   **Explanation:** This sentence requires parallel structure with gerunds, so "trying" aligns with "traveling."

3. **Correction:** "The results of the survey, *which was conducted last year,* were released yesterday."

    o   **Explanation:** Remove redundancy by deleting "it," and ensure the verb tense agrees.

Key Points to Remember

1. **Identify the Question Type Quickly:** Distinguish between grammar, structure, and style to target your analysis effectively.

2. **Use Process of Elimination:** Remove incorrect choices strategically to narrow down options.

3. **Balance Speed and Accuracy with Practice:** Gradual increases in timed practice help you achieve efficient yet accurate responses.

4. **Set Aside Time for Review:** Save a few minutes to revisit flagged questions and recheck common grammatical issues.

By mastering these techniques, you'll be well-prepared to handle the SAT Writing and Language section confidently. Through targeted practice, quick analysis, and efficient time management, you'll develop the skills to answer with precision even under the pressure of the test timer. With each practice session, you're moving closer to achieving high accuracy and building the confidence needed to excel on test day.

Chapter 6: Boosting Your SAT Scores with Advanced Strategies

6.1 Score-Boosting Strategies for Math

In this subchapter, we delve into advanced strategies tailored to help you handle the toughest math questions on the Digital SAT. These are high-impact techniques designed to give you a competitive edge by enhancing both accuracy and efficiency. From refining elimination methods to honing educated guessing skills and mastering complex problem-solving approaches, each strategy equips you to face challenging math questions with confidence.

Leveraging the Process of Elimination to Narrow Down Answers

The process of elimination is a powerful technique that allows you to reduce choices systematically, boosting both your accuracy and speed. For many multiple-choice questions, eliminating improbable answers before solving can simplify the problem significantly.

Step-by-Step Guide to Effective Elimination

1. **First, Spot the Impossibilities**
   Start by identifying answer choices that are clearly incorrect. For example, if the question involves positive numbers and some answer

choices are negative, you can immediately rule those out. Similarly, if a question is asking for a minimum or maximum value, eliminate answers that don't logically fit within that range.

- o **Example:**
  - Question: "Which of the following could be the solution for $x^2=16$?"
  - Choices: (A) 4, (B) -4, (C) 0, (D) 5
  - **Solution:** Eliminate (C) and (D) immediately, as they don't satisfy $x^2=16$. The correct choices are (A) and (B), giving you two viable options to consider.

2. **Estimate and Approximate When Possible**
   For questions that involve lengthy calculations, use estimation to narrow down the choices. For instance, in geometry questions, if you have rough measurements, apply these to approximate potential answers.

- o **Example:**
  - Question: "A circle has a radius of approximately 7. What is its approximate area?"
  - Choices: (A) 44, (B) 77, (C) 154, (D) 200
  - **Solution:** Since the area is calculated as $\pi r^2 \approx 3.14 \times 7^2 \approx 154$, eliminate anything too far from 154, leaving (C) as the correct answer.

3. **Plug in Answer Choices to Verify**
   For algebraic questions, plug in each answer choice to see if it satisfies the equation. This technique works well when the question has answer choices that can be substituted back into the problem.

- o **Example:**
  - Question: "If $4x+8=24$, what is the value of x?"
  - Solution: Start by substituting values from the choices into the equation until you find the one that satisfies $4x+8=24$.

Challenge Exercise: Apply elimination to this problem:

- "A box contains 4 blue balls, 3 red balls, and 5 green balls. What is the probability of drawing a blue ball?"

  o Choices: (A) 1/12, (B) 1/3, (C) 2/3, (D) 1/2

  o **Solution:** The probability is calculated as $\frac{4}{12} = \frac{1}{3}$. Eliminate options that don't match this logic, confirming that (B) is correct.

Implementing Educated Guessing Techniques to Enhance Accuracy

When you're uncertain of the answer but have narrowed down options, educated guessing can be a powerful scoring strategy. Since the SAT doesn't penalize for incorrect answers, this approach lets you boost your odds of success without risking points.

Techniques for Smart Guessing

1. **Eliminate Choices Systematically**
   First, eliminate choices you know are incorrect. Even if you're down to two potential answers, your odds are now 50/50—a substantial improvement over random guessing among all choices.

2. **Consider Numerical Patterns**
   Some questions, particularly in algebra and arithmetic, have answer choices that follow certain patterns. For example, if a question about probability lists fractions as answers, consider whether the denominator makes sense within the context of the problem (e.g., total items or outcomes).

3. **Look at Answer Range and Outliers**
   When answer choices include an extreme outlier, it's often safe to discard it, as SAT questions generally don't include unreasonably high or low options. Focus on options that fit within a logical range.

   o **Example:**

     - Question: "The approximate value of $\sqrt{60}$ is?"

     - Choices: (A) 6, (B) 7.5, (C) 8, (D) 15

     - **Solution:** Since $\sqrt{49}=7$ and $\sqrt{64}=8$, the best approximation is (C) 8.

4. **Backsolve by Testing Choices in the Original Equation**
   Substitute answer choices back into the question to see if they work logically. This approach is particularly helpful in word problems, inequalities, or when dealing with equations involving specific values.

Challenge Exercise: Try educated guessing on this question:

- "If 40% of a number is 80, what is the number?"

  o Choices: (A) 120, (B) 160, (C) 200, (D) 240

  o **Solution**: Recognizing that 40% is the same as $0.4x=80$, solving gives $x=200$, making (C) the correct answer.

Mastering Open-Ended Math Questions with Advanced Techniques

Open-ended questions on the SAT require precise calculation and a strong understanding of math concepts. Here's how to approach them effectively.

Key Approaches for Open-Ended Questions

1. **Break the Problem into Parts**
   When you encounter complex questions, break them down into manageable parts. Tackling each segment individually can prevent you from feeling overwhelmed and lead to a more organized solution.

   o **Example:**

     ▪ Question: "If $3x - 5 = 16$, what is the value of x?"

     ▪ Solution: Add 5 to both sides, yielding $3x=21$, then divide by 3 to find $x=7$.

2. **Estimate and Refine**
   For questions involving fractions, square roots, or percentages, make a rough estimate first. Then, refine your answer based on the options provided. Estimation is especially helpful with word problems or geometry questions involving large or complex numbers.

3. **Use Reverse Engineering or Backtracking**
   Some open-ended questions give you the outcome, asking you to determine the initial value. In such cases, work backward through the operations in the problem.

   o **Example:**

- Question: "If a number is doubled and then increased by 6 to yield 20, what is the original number?"

- Solution: Reverse the steps: 20 - 6 = 14, then divide by 2 to get the original number as 7.

Challenge Exercise: Solve this open-ended question:

- "What is the value of y if 5y+15=50?"

    o **Solution**: Subtract 15 from both sides to get 5y=35, then divide by 5 to find y=7.

Efficiency Strategies for Tackling Complex Math Questions

When faced with particularly difficult questions, managing your time and energy effectively is essential. Here are strategies to streamline your approach.

Time-Saving Techniques for Challenging Questions

1. **Skip and Revisit**
   If a question seems overly complex, don't waste too much time on it right away. Move on and return if time allows. This strategy ensures you accumulate points on easier questions before tackling the harder ones.

2. **Approximate in Lengthy Calculations**
   Approximation helps speed up calculations in questions involving large numbers, square roots, or decimals. Simplify calculations to manageable estimates, then adjust if needed.

    o **Example**: If a question asks for $\pi \times 49$, approximate $\pi \approx 3$ to get 3 x 49 = 147, which is close enough for estimation.

3. **Draw or Visualize**
   Visualization is crucial for geometry questions or any problem that can be represented graphically. Draw out shapes, label measurements, or diagram the problem whenever possible to clarify relationships and reduce errors.

    o **Example**: For a question about triangle sides and angles, sketching the triangle with given dimensions often makes solving easier.

4. **Simplify Units and Values Early On**

   If the question involves units (like inches and feet) or complex fractions, convert or simplify early in the problem. This step makes the math easier as you progress through the question.

Complex Question Practice

Practice applying these efficiency techniques to the following complex question:

- "A triangle has two sides measuring 5 and 12. What is the possible range for the third side?"

  o Solution: Use the triangle inequality theorem: the sum of any two sides must be greater than the third side. The range is $7 < x < 17$.

Interactive Practice: "Challenge Yourself"

Try these additional questions using the techniques discussed above. Focus on refining your approach to elimination, educated guessing, and open-ended problem-solving.

Challenge Questions:

1. "If $3x+9=27$, what is the value of x?"

   o Solution: Subtract 9 from both sides, giving $3x=18$, then divide by 3 to get $x=6$.

2. "In a survey of 50 students, 30 are studying math, 20 are studying science, and 10 are studying both. How many students are studying only one subject?"

   o Solution: Use set theory (Venn diagram). Math-only students: $30 - 10 = 20$, Science-only: $20 - 10 = 10$, so total is $20 + 10 = 30$.

3. "A rectangle has a length twice its width. If its perimeter is 36, what are its dimensions?"

   o Solution: Let width = x, length = 2x. Perimeter formula: $2(x+2x)=36$. Solving gives $x=6$, so dimensions are 6 and 12.

By mastering these score-boosting strategies for math, you'll be equipped to handle the most challenging SAT questions with confidence and accuracy. With regular practice, these techniques will become second nature, allowing you to tackle each question efficiently and maximize your score potential on test day.

6.2 Mastering Reading with Advanced Techniques

The Digital SAT Reading section demands not only comprehension skills but also a keen ability to navigate complex passages, discern distractors, and handle challenging vocabulary. In this subchapter, we dive into advanced strategies that empower you to tackle tricky questions and misleading answer choices with precision. By developing techniques for identifying distractors, utilizing context clues for vocabulary, and analyzing challenging passages effectively, you'll enhance your accuracy, speed, and confidence.

Identifying Trick Questions and Distractors

Many SAT Reading questions are designed with answer choices that can easily lead you astray. These "distractors" often sound plausible or mimic language from the passage but subtly miss the main idea or key detail.

Techniques for Recognizing Distractors

1. **Look for Keywords in the Question**
    Pay close attention to the question wording and keywords. Common keywords like "best supports," "main purpose," and "primarily" focus the question. Distractor answers may use words from the passage without addressing these keywords directly.

    o   **Example:**

        ▪   Passage Context: An author discusses the importance of renewable energy for sustainability.

        ▪   Question: "What is the primary purpose of the passage?"

        ▪   Distractor Answer: "To discuss the challenges of fossil fuels."

- **Explanation**: While the passage may mention fossil fuels, the primary purpose is to emphasize renewable energy.

2. **Be Cautious with "Extreme" Language**
   Distractors often use extreme language, such as "always," "never," "all," or "none." These answers are typically incorrect in SAT Reading because they don't accurately reflect the nuanced nature of the passages.

3. **Match Tone and Scope**
   The SAT often includes answers that, while factually correct, do not match the passage's tone or scope. For example, if a passage discusses a topic in a balanced way, an answer choice that presents an overly positive or negative view is likely a distractor.

4. **Avoid Overlapping Language Traps**
   Some distractors reuse words from the passage to make an answer seem relevant. However, simply sharing vocabulary with the text doesn't make the answer correct. Focus on the main idea and context rather than specific words.

Challenge for You:

- Try applying these techniques to this sample question:

  o Question: "The author's primary concern in the passage is to highlight…"

    - (A) the challenges of implementing new technologies

    - (B) the potential benefits of renewable energy

    - (C) the environmental impact of industrial activities

    - (D) the need for international policy changes

  o **Solution**: Focus on the main idea of the passage and eliminate options that don't address the author's main concern. Correct answer: (B).

Using Context Clues to Solve Vocabulary Questions

Vocabulary questions on the SAT require you to understand the meaning of words based on the context in which they're used. These questions are less about knowing definitions and more about deducing meaning from the surrounding text.

Steps for Interpreting Vocabulary in Context

1. **Identify Clues in Nearby Sentences**
   Words, phrases, or descriptions near the targeted word often give clues to its meaning. Look for synonyms, antonyms, or examples within the passage that suggest the word's definition.

2. **Pay Attention to Transition Words**
   Transition words like "however," "similarly," and "in contrast" help indicate whether the word is meant to align with or differ from nearby information.

   o **Example:**

      ▪ Passage: "While some argue that renewable energy is costly, it is actually *sustainable* in the long run."

      ▪ Question: In this context, "sustainable" most likely means...

         ▪ Choices: (A) short-term, (B) dependable, (C) profitable, (D) enduring

         ▪ **Solution**: The contrast with "costly" suggests something lasting or worthwhile, so (D) enduring is correct.

3. **Consider the Word's Function in the Sentence**
   Sometimes, analyzing whether a word is used as a noun, verb, adjective, etc., can clarify its meaning. For instance, "aesthetic" used as a noun vs. adjective can imply slightly different meanings.

4. **Use Logical Substitution**
   Substitute each answer choice back into the sentence. Select the one that makes the most logical sense given the context.

Practice Exercise:

- Passage Sentence: "The scientist's discovery was considered *novel*, sparking interest among peers."

   o Question: As used in the passage, "novel" most nearly means...

- (A) strange, (B) original, (C) common, (D) unclear

  o **Solution:** The context suggests interest due to newness or uniqueness, so (B) original is correct.

Analyzing Difficult Passages Efficiently

Reading complex passages requires skills in organizing information, connecting ideas, and understanding nuances. By approaching difficult texts with a structured analysis method, you can enhance comprehension and minimize confusion.

Techniques for Efficient Passage Analysis

1. **Identify the Passage Structure**
   Most SAT passages follow a structure that begins with an introduction, develops ideas with evidence, and concludes with a summary or statement of purpose. Recognizing this pattern can help you anticipate the author's main points.

2. **Focus on the First and Last Sentences of Paragraphs**
   The main idea of each paragraph often lies in its first sentence, while the last sentence may provide a concluding or transitional statement. This method saves time by letting you grasp the main points without reading every word.

3. **Track Key Themes and Transitions**
   Notice transitions in tone or argument, often signaled by words like "however," "in addition," or "on the other hand." These shifts indicate shifts in the author's argument or additional details that refine the main idea.

4. **Underline or Note Important Concepts**
   As you read, underline (if allowed) or mentally note key names, dates, or concepts that the passage emphasizes. These details often reappear in questions and are crucial for accuracy.

5. **Avoid Over-Reading into Details**
   The SAT requires you to understand central ideas and evidence—not minor details. Stay focused on the broader argument rather than getting lost in specific examples or technical details.

Challenge for You:

- Read the following sample passage and try to identify its main idea.

  o Passage: "While many have criticized renewable energy for being costly, studies have shown it provides long-term benefits to both the environment and the economy."

  o Main Idea Question: What is the author's primary assertion?

    ▪ Answer Choices:

        ▪ (A) Renewable energy has significant short-term costs.

        ▪ (B) Renewable energy benefits the environment and economy in the long term.

        ▪ (C) Critics believe renewable energy is beneficial.

        ▪ (D) Renewable energy has no economic impact.

  o **Solution**: The passage emphasizes long-term benefits, so (B) is correct.

Interactive Section: "Challenge Yourself"

In this section, apply the advanced techniques discussed in this chapter to the following questions. These exercises reinforce your ability to identify distractors, deduce vocabulary, and efficiently analyze passages.

Challenge Questions:

1. **Distractor Identification**
   Passage Excerpt: "The author argues that while implementing renewable energy solutions may require significant investment, the benefits far outweigh the initial costs."

   o Question: "What is the main argument presented by the author?"

       ▪ (A) Renewable energy is too expensive to implement.

- (B) The initial investment in renewable energy is justified by long-term benefits.

- (C) Renewable energy benefits the environment but harms the economy.

- (D) Initial costs are minimal for renewable energy.

   o **Solution**: The author emphasizes that benefits outweigh initial costs, making (B) the best answer.

2. **Vocabulary in Context**
   Passage Sentence: "Her approach to problem-solving was unconventional, yet it yielded impressive results."

   o Question: As used in the sentence, "unconventional" most nearly means…

   - (A) unusual, (B) cautious, (C) standard, (D) random

   o **Solution**: The positive outcome suggests "unconventional" as a non-traditional approach, making (A) unusual correct.

3. **Efficient Passage Analysis**
   Passage Overview: "The author explores the impact of plastic pollution on marine life, emphasizing both the immediate and long-term consequences."

   o Main Idea Question: "What does the author emphasize in the passage?"

   - (A) The benefits of plastic in industrial applications.

   - (B) Immediate effects of pollution on marine life.

   - (C) Both immediate and lasting impacts of plastic pollution.

   - (D) Solutions to the pollution problem.

   o **Solution**: The author discusses both immediate and long-term consequences, so (C) is correct.

By mastering these advanced reading techniques, you'll be prepared to tackle challenging SAT passages with skill and accuracy. Regular practice with these methods will make recognizing distractors, interpreting vocabulary, and analyzing complex texts feel like second nature. With each practice session, you're developing the confidence and insight needed to excel in the SAT Reading section.

6.3 Efficient Use of Time in All Sections

The ability to manage time efficiently is a game-changer for achieving high scores on the Digital SAT. Each section of the SAT comes with its own set of timing challenges, and learning to allocate your time wisely, avoid second-guessing, and navigate skipped questions can lead to a significant improvement in your overall performance.

Managing Your Time Across Sections to Maximize Your Score

Each section of the SAT has a different pace requirement, and understanding how to distribute your time in each one can make all the difference. Here's a breakdown of optimal time management for each section:

1. **Math Section**

   o In the Math section, balance between speed and accuracy is key, especially in more challenging problem-solving and grid-in questions. Spend no more than **1 minute on easy questions** and **about 2 minutes on more complex problems**.

   o **Example**: If there are 30 questions to answer in 60 minutes, you should allocate around 1–2 minutes per question. If you encounter a particularly difficult question, flag it, move on, and return to it if time allows.

2. **Reading Section**

   o For the Reading section, each passage should take **about 10-12 minutes**, including the questions associated with it. Break down your time by spending **3-5 minutes reading and annotating the passage** and the remaining time answering questions.

   o **Example Strategy**: Spend the first minute skimming the passage to identify main ideas and structure. Focus on understanding the author's argument and the passage's tone to answer questions efficiently without rereading.

3. **Writing and Language Section**

   o Each question here requires careful reading, but time per question should be **about 30–40 seconds**. Try reading through each sentence fully before answering grammar or syntax questions.

   o **Example:** If you have 44 questions in 35 minutes, aim to complete each question in under a minute, marking any complex sentences that may need a second look and returning to them at the end.

Techniques for Reducing Second-Guessing and Sticking to Your Answers

One of the biggest challenges in any timed test is resisting the urge to second-guess your answers, which can waste precious time. Here are techniques to avoid overthinking and confidently stick with your first choice:

1. **Trust Your Gut**
   Studies show that your first instinct is often correct. Unless you have a concrete reason to change an answer, go with your initial response. If you start second-guessing, remind yourself that overthinking can lead to lower accuracy.

2. **Avoid Over-Rereading**
   For the Reading and Writing sections, over-rereading the passage or question can lead to unnecessary doubts. Instead, focus on understanding the main idea the first time you read it and trust your interpretation. Mark questions you're unsure about to revisit if time allows.

3. **Use Process of Elimination**
   Eliminating incorrect answers first helps you feel more confident in your final selection. Once you've narrowed it down to two choices, pick the option that best aligns with the question and move on without lingering.

4. **Practice Confident Decision-Making**
   Confidence builds through practice. In your study sessions, set a

timer and train yourself to make quick, decisive choices. This habit translates well on test day, allowing you to maximize your score by staying within the time limit.

Challenge for You:

- Apply these strategies to a short reading passage or a set of math questions. Practice choosing an answer without changing it and note if your initial choices were accurate.

Reviewing Skipped Questions Without Wasting Time

Skipped questions are a reality in the SAT, and the trick is to review them effectively without spending too long. Here's how to approach skipped questions to maximize your scoring potential:

1. **Prioritize Skipped Questions**
   As you review skipped questions, tackle easier ones first. This gives you a confidence boost and ensures you're gaining as many points as possible without spending too much time on one difficult question.

2. **Use the Clock Wisely**
   Set a limit for each skipped question review. If you're nearing the end of the section, give each skipped question about 30 seconds before making a final decision. If you still can't decide, use educated guessing rather than leaving it blank.

3. **Apply Context Clues in Reading and Writing**
   For skipped questions in the Reading and Writing sections, use context clues to quickly jog your memory on the passage or grammar rule. Revisiting each sentence or paragraph could waste time, so try to recall the main point or rule.

4. **Revisit Math Steps for Accuracy**
   In the Math section, retrace your steps on skipped questions to identify where the error might have occurred. Avoid reworking the entire problem from scratch unless necessary. Instead, focus on rechecking calculations or revisiting the main setup of the problem.

Example:
If you skipped a question in the Reading section, start by reviewing the part of the passage directly relevant to the question. For math, retrace only the part where you were initially uncertain (e.g., a calculation or formula application).

Interactive Section: "Challenge Yourself"

Use the following challenge questions to put these time management strategies into action. Focus on maintaining a steady pace and avoiding second-guessing as you move through each question.

Challenge Questions:

1. **Reading Section Example**
   Passage: "The author argues that renewable energy, while initially expensive, offers substantial long-term benefits."

   o Question: What is the main point of the passage?

      ▪ (A) Renewable energy is too costly to consider.

      ▪ (B) Renewable energy's benefits outweigh its costs.

      ▪ (C) Renewable energy is primarily about environmental impact.

      ▪ (D) The author is uncertain about renewable energy's benefits.

   o **Solution**: (B). Select the answer confidently without second-guessing, focusing on the main idea as you read.

2. **Math Section Example**
   Question: "If $2x+5=15$, what is the value of x?"

   o Solution:

      ▪ Step 1: Subtract 5 from both sides: $2x=10$.

      ▪ Step 2: Divide by 2: $x=5$.

      ▪ **Tip**: Set a time limit of 1 minute for this type of question and avoid rechecking if your steps were accurate.

3. **Writing and Language Section Example**
   Question: Choose the correct word to complete the sentence: "The committee was ___ by the unexpected results of the study."

   o Choices: (A) elated, (B) surprised, (C) angered, (D) distracted

- o **Solution:** (B) surprised best fits the neutral tone of a study outcome.

With these time management strategies, you'll improve not only your pacing across the SAT but also your accuracy by avoiding the common pitfalls of overthinking and excessive reviewing. With regular practice, these techniques will become second nature, helping you achieve your highest potential score on test day.

6.4 Strategic Use of Practice Tests for Score Improvement

Practice tests are one of the most powerful tools you can use to improve your SAT score. By analyzing both strengths and weaknesses, setting score goals, and refining your approach to each section, practice tests help transform weaknesses into strengths and bring you closer to your target score. In this subchapter, we'll go through strategies for making practice tests a core part of your preparation.

Using Practice Tests to Identify High-Yield Areas for Improvement

When taking practice tests, it's essential to identify which question types and content areas yield the most significant improvements with targeted practice. Focus on understanding where you can gain the most points in the shortest time.

Steps to Pinpoint High-Yield Areas

1. **Track Question Types You Struggle With**
   After each practice test, review the questions you answered incorrectly and categorize them by topic. For instance, in the Math section, note if most of your errors are in algebra, geometry, or problem-solving. For Reading, assess if inference questions or main idea questions are more challenging.

   - o **Example:** If you find that you're missing questions on geometry consistently, prioritize this topic in your study sessions.

2. **Identify Patterns in Mistakes**
   Sometimes, mistakes are due to time constraints, second-guessing, or

misinterpreting the question rather than knowledge gaps. Identifying the underlying reason for errors can help tailor your preparation. If you frequently change correct answers to incorrect ones, focus on building confidence in your first instincts.

3. **Set Priorities Based on Improvement Potential**
   Once you've pinpointed the high-yield areas, prioritize these topics in your study plan. Allocate more time to these sections, as gains in these areas will likely have a significant impact on your overall score.

Setting Score Goals and Tracking Incremental Progress

Setting a specific score goal provides motivation and a clear target for your efforts. However, incremental progress is key to reaching that goal steadily, keeping you motivated along the way.

Steps for Effective Goal-Setting and Progress Tracking

1. **Establish a Realistic Score Goal**
   Based on your current score, set an achievable goal for each practice test phase. If your initial score is 1200 and your target is 1400, plan for gradual increases, aiming for 1300 first before pushing higher.

2. **Break Down Goals by Section**
   Setting section-specific targets helps you focus on particular areas needing improvement. For instance, aim for a 50-point improvement in Math first, followed by a 30-point boost in Reading.

3. **Track Your Scores and Adjust as Needed**
   Create a tracking sheet or use a spreadsheet to log each practice test score, recording details for each section. Over time, patterns emerge, and you can adjust your study focus based on these results.

4. **Reward Incremental Achievements**
   Celebrating small wins is essential to stay motivated. Reward yourself when you hit milestones, whether it's improving in one section or achieving a higher overall score than your last attempt.

Challenge for You:

- Set a realistic score target for your next practice test, and break it down by section. After completing the test, evaluate your performance in each area and adjust your target for the next round.

Analyzing Both Correct and Incorrect Answers to Improve Accuracy

A thorough review of both correct and incorrect answers will help you refine your approach, ensuring that you don't just memorize answers but truly understand the reasoning behind each choice.

How to Conduct a Comprehensive Review

1. **Review Incorrect Answers for Patterns**
   Identify why you missed each question—was it due to misunderstanding the question, a careless error, or a lack of knowledge? Understanding the cause of each mistake helps you implement specific strategies to avoid repeating the error.

2. **Examine Correct Answers for Reinforcement**
   Even for correct answers, review the logic you used to arrive at the answer. This reinforcement helps you understand which strategies are working and builds confidence in your approach.

3. **Focus on Process, Not Just Content**
   Rather than just noting which questions were right or wrong, focus on the process you used. Were you guessing? Did you eliminate distractors effectively? Reflecting on your process will help you refine strategies across future practice tests.

4. **Note Any Timing Issues**
   Track which questions took you the longest. Questions that consistently exceed your ideal time limit may require targeted practice to improve speed or efficiency. This insight can lead to adjustments in pacing strategies.

Example:

- If you find that Reading section inference questions consistently slow you down, focus on inference practice. This can involve practicing with shorter passages, timing yourself, and reviewing only inference questions until you gain speed.

Interactive Section: "Challenge Yourself"

Apply these techniques to your next practice test to enhance your learning and maximize improvement.

Challenge Exercises:

1. **Identify High-Yield Areas**
   After your practice test, categorize each missed question by topic. Highlight the top two areas where you missed the most questions, and create a focused plan to address these topics.

2. **Set a Realistic Goal for the Next Test**
   Use your latest score as a baseline. Set a clear score goal for each section, and track your progress. Evaluate your improvement areas in the next test and adjust goals based on the results.

3. **Analyze Correct and Incorrect Answers**
   Review both correct and incorrect answers from your latest practice test. Write down the logic behind your correct answers and identify any patterns in missed questions. Focus on improving these specific areas in your next study session.

6.5 Boosting Confidence Before Test Day

Mental preparation is as vital as academic preparation for achieving a high score on the SAT. Cultivating a calm, confident mindset not only reduces test-day anxiety but also enhances performance, allowing you to tackle even the most challenging questions with clarity and focus. In this subchapter, you'll learn powerful techniques to build confidence, manage stress, and enter the exam room with a positive, resilient mindset.

Mental Strategies for Reducing Test Anxiety

Test anxiety is common, but with effective strategies, you can minimize it and perform at your best. Anxiety can lead to self-doubt and wasted mental energy, so developing tools to manage it will significantly improve your test-day experience.

Techniques for Reducing Anxiety

1. **Practice Deep Breathing**
   Deep breathing is one of the most accessible and effective ways to manage anxiety. Before starting each section, take a few deep breaths to reset your mind and body. A simple breathing exercise is the "4-7-

8" method: inhale for 4 seconds, hold for 7, and exhale for 8. This calms your nervous system, reducing tension.

2. **Use Positive Self-Talk**
Replace negative thoughts ("I'm not ready" or "What if I fail?") with empowering ones. Remind yourself of the effort you've put into studying and that you have the tools you need to succeed. Repeat affirmations such as "I am prepared and focused" or "I can handle any challenge."

3. **Visualize a Positive Outcome**
Visualize yourself successfully navigating each section of the SAT, remaining calm, and answering questions confidently. Picture yourself completing the test feeling proud of your effort. Visualization techniques help create a positive mindset and reduce fear of the unknown.

4. **Prepare for Small Breaks Between Sections**
During official breaks, use simple stretches or quick breathing exercises to release tension. This will keep your body relaxed and your mind sharp as you transition between sections.

Challenge for You:

- Before each study session, try using the "4-7-8" breathing technique to calm your mind. After a week, note any changes in your focus and anxiety levels during practice tests.

Positive Visualization Techniques to Enhance Performance

Visualization is a powerful tool to enhance confidence and prepare mentally for high-stakes situations. By picturing a successful outcome, you can train your mind to respond calmly and focus on achieving your best.

Steps for Effective Visualization

1. **Create a Detailed Mental Image**
Picture the testing environment—arriving at the test center, opening the test booklet, and confidently approaching each question. Imagine yourself working through the exam with ease, maintaining a steady rhythm, and managing time effectively.

2. **Focus on Key Moments**

   Break down the visualization into specific moments, like starting each section with clarity, tackling a tough question calmly, or finishing with time to spare. This reinforces a sense of control and reduces uncertainty.

3. **Incorporate All Senses**

   Visualization is most effective when you use all your senses. Imagine how the test room sounds, how the chair feels, even the texture of the pencil in your hand. By making the experience as realistic as possible, you help desensitize yourself to test-day stressors.

4. **Visualize Daily for Consistency**

   Practice this visualization daily for at least 5 minutes. The goal is to make it a routine part of your preparation. Over time, your mind becomes accustomed to seeing a positive outcome, reinforcing self-confidence.

Example:

- Every evening, take 5 minutes to visualize the entire SAT test day in as much detail as possible. See yourself approaching the test with calm confidence, fully prepared for each section.

Preparing for Success with a Positive Mindset

A positive mindset is the foundation of test-day success. The right mental state boosts focus, resilience, and problem-solving abilities. Here's how to cultivate a mindset geared toward success.

Steps to Building a Positive Mindset

1. **Develop a Pre-Test Routine**

   A structured routine the day before and the morning of the test will help you stay grounded and focused. This could include a balanced meal, light exercise, and a quick review of affirmations or goals. Routines reduce the risk of last-minute stress.

2. **Focus on What You Can Control**

   Instead of worrying about uncontrollable factors (such as specific questions you'll face), focus on aspects within your control: your preparation, your response to challenges, and your mental state. This shift empowers you and keeps you centered.

3. **Create and Review Affirmations**
   Write down a list of positive affirmations tailored to the SAT, such as "I am ready for this challenge" or "I am skilled at managing my time." Read through them every morning to reinforce a positive mindset and reinforce your self-belief.

4. **Reflect on Past Successes**
   Remind yourself of past achievements, whether in school or extracurriculars, where you performed well despite challenges. This builds confidence in your ability to handle pressure.

5. **Reframe Negative Thoughts**
   When doubts arise, challenge and replace them with constructive ones. Instead of "I might fail," say, "I have prepared well, and I am capable." This shift helps redirect energy toward productive thinking.

Challenge for You:

- Write a list of 5 personal affirmations related to your SAT goals. Read them daily in the week leading up to the test, paying attention to any changes in your confidence levels.

Interactive Section: "Challenge Yourself"

Use these interactive exercises to practice building a positive mindset, managing anxiety, and visualizing success.

Challenge Exercises:

1. **Breathing Exercise Practice**

   o Spend 5 minutes practicing the "4-7-8" breathing method before each study session this week. Track any differences in focus or stress levels after the session.

2. **Visualization Exercise**

   o Close your eyes and visualize yourself succeeding on the SAT. Imagine specific moments, such as confidently starting each section, calmly approaching difficult questions, and finishing the test. Repeat daily to reinforce positive expectations.

3. **Affirmation Creation and Review**

o   Create a list of affirmations that address your SAT goals. For example, "I am focused and prepared," or "I have the skills to excel in every section." Review these affirmations every morning to build confidence and focus.

By integrating these mental strategies, you'll prepare not only your knowledge but also your mindset for the SAT. Building a positive, resilient mindset allows you to handle challenges with confidence, ensuring that you walk into test day prepared, composed, and ready to perform at your best.

Chapter 7: Staying Motivated and Resilient Throughout Your SAT Journey

7.1 Setting Long-Term Goals for Success

Setting goals is not just about defining what you want; it's about creating a path to get there. In this first step of your journey to SAT success, you'll learn the art of setting effective, long-term goals and breaking them down into manageable steps. The objective? To stay motivated, resilient, and on track. We'll guide you through goal-setting methods, introduce reward systems, and share stories of students who achieved their SAT goals through commitment and strategy.

Defining and Visualizing Your Final SAT Score Goal

The journey begins with a vision. What's your target score? Imagine the moment when you see your SAT score, one that reflects the hard work and hours of preparation you've invested. Visualization isn't just wishful thinking—it's a powerful mental tool that primes your mind for success and keeps you focused. Studies have shown that imagining success can significantly boost motivation and commitment, as your brain starts believing in the possibility of that outcome.

Reflection Question: What does achieving your SAT goal mean to you personally? How will it impact your college applications, your future? Take a moment to picture this vividly.

Breaking Down Long-Term Goals into Smaller, Achievable Milestones

A high SAT score is an ambitious goal, but it can feel overwhelming when viewed as a single, monumental task. By breaking down your SAT goal into smaller, achievable milestones, you transform it from a daunting challenge into a series of manageable steps. Think of these milestones as checkpoints on your journey, each bringing you closer to your ultimate goal.

Consider **Daniel's Story**. Daniel set a goal to score 1400 on the SAT. Rather than focusing solely on the final number, he broke it down. In his first month, his milestone was to improve his math score by 50 points. He achieved this by focusing on problem areas, like algebra. Celebrating this progress motivated him to tackle his next milestone in reading comprehension.

Here's how you can do it:

1. **Set clear milestones** for each section of the SAT. For example, "Improve Math by 50 points" or "Increase Reading speed by 10 words per minute."

2. **Track your progress regularly,** such as by taking practice tests every two weeks. Measure your improvements in each section to see how you're advancing.

3. **Celebrate small wins**. When you hit a milestone, take a moment to recognize your progress. Maybe treat yourself to a small reward—a favorite snack, a break day, or a relaxing activity you love.

Challenge for You: Write down your SAT goal, then break it down into monthly or weekly targets. Focus on one area for each target and track how these incremental steps move you closer to the score you want.

Keeping Motivation High with Reward Systems and Progress Tracking

Staying motivated over the weeks or months of SAT prep can be difficult. That's where a reward system and progress tracking come in.

Reward Systems

Rewards don't have to be extravagant. Even small incentives can make a big difference. Rewards can boost your dopamine levels, the chemical associated with pleasure and motivation, making the process of studying more enjoyable.

Example: Mia decided to reward herself with a movie night whenever she completed three straight weeks of her study plan. These mini-rewards helped her sustain a steady pace, as she always had something positive to look forward to after each study period.

Suggestions for Building Your Reward System:

- **Small rewards for weekly goals**: A favorite snack, a night out with friends, or a new book.

- **Medium rewards for monthly milestones**: A weekend outing, a new item, or a hobby day.

- **A larger reward for achieving your final score goal**: A meaningful purchase, a short trip, or an activity you've always wanted to try.

Reflection Question: What small reward can you give yourself at the end of this week for staying consistent with your study goals?

Progress Tracking

Tracking progress allows you to see how far you've come and how close you are to your final goal. You can use a physical journal, an app, or a spreadsheet to record your scores, time spent studying, and areas for improvement.

Here's how to create a tracking system:

1. **Set a baseline** by taking a practice test and recording your initial scores in each section.

2. **Track scores regularly** to see growth over time. For instance, record your scores weekly to monitor areas that need more attention.

3. **Reflect on your progress** every month. What strategies worked best? What topics do you still need to focus on?

Interactive Section: Challenge for You

Set a mini-goal for yourself this week. For example, "I will study for the SAT Math section for 1 hour, three days this week." After each session, check off your progress. At the end of the week, reward yourself for completing the mini-goal, and reflect on how it feels to take a tangible step toward your larger SAT goal.

Key Takeaways:

- **Visualize your goal**: A clear picture of success helps keep you motivated.

- **Break down your big goal** into smaller steps to stay focused and avoid burnout.

- **Reward yourself** for progress, however small, to keep morale high.

- **Track your achievements** to remind yourself how far you've come and to adjust as needed.

Success Story: Sarah's Journey to a Higher Score

Sarah aimed for a 1350 SAT score but started with 1000. By setting specific, smaller goals, like "Improve by 10 points in Math each month," she reached 1300 by test day. With each mini-milestone, her confidence grew, showing her that success is a series of small, consistent steps. Her determination was fueled by a balanced mix of progress tracking and rewards.

By setting goals, rewarding yourself, and tracking progress, you're building a roadmap that makes success achievable and realistic. As you complete each step, remember that each milestone reached is a testament to your hard work and commitment, bringing you closer to achieving the score you desire. Keep moving forward with confidence—you're capable of reaching your SAT dreams!

7.2 Dealing with Setbacks and Maintaining Confidence

Everyone encounters obstacles along the path to success, and the SAT journey is no different. This chapter is dedicated to helping you handle setbacks with resilience, build confidence, and turn challenges into opportunities for growth. You'll learn practical strategies to navigate low practice scores, mental techniques to strengthen your resolve, and inspiring success stories that remind you: progress is possible, no matter the setbacks.

How to Handle Low Practice Test Scores and Improve

You've put in hours of study, but the latest practice test score is less than you hoped for. It's easy to feel disappointed, but remember—this score doesn't define your final result. Each low score is a learning opportunity and a stepping stone toward improvement.

Reflection Question: When faced with a score that doesn't meet your expectations, what is your initial reaction? Do you feel discouraged, or do you see it as a sign to reassess your approach?

Think of **Emma's Story.** Emma aimed for a 1450 on the SAT, but her initial practice tests came in around 1200. She realized that instead of giving in to frustration, she could use these scores to identify her weak areas. She focused on improving in math and increased her score incrementally, one section at a time. By the end of her journey, Emma had reached her target.

Strategies for Handling Low Scores:

1. **Analyze your test results.** Identify areas where you lost points and the types of questions that were most challenging.

2. **Adjust your study plan** based on your analysis. Focus more on weaker areas without neglecting your strengths.

3. **Seek extra help if needed.** Resources like tutors, study groups, or online courses can provide the targeted assistance you may need.

4. **Practice under test conditions.** Familiarize yourself with the pressure of real testing situations by timing your practice and simulating the environment.

Challenge for You: After your next practice test, take a deep breath, and write down three specific areas to work on based on your mistakes. Then, make a mini-plan to address each one in the following week.

Building Resilience in the Face of Setbacks

Resilience is your ability to bounce back stronger after each setback. Rather than letting challenges define your journey, view them as moments that build your inner strength. Resilient students don't avoid setbacks—they overcome them.

Consider Liam's Experience. Liam struggled with reading comprehension, often feeling disheartened after practice tests. But instead of focusing on each disappointing score, he started visualizing his growth. Each time he encountered a low score, he noted the specific areas that needed work. Eventually, he saw steady improvement and built a habit of resilience that extended beyond the SAT.

Resilience-Building Techniques:

- **Reframe setbacks as learning opportunities**. Every low score provides valuable feedback on what needs attention.

- **Practice self-compassion**. Instead of being critical of yourself, acknowledge your hard work and progress.

- **Set realistic expectations**. Remember that improvement is gradual. Recognize even small progress as a victory.

- **Develop a "growth mindset"**. Believe that abilities can be developed through dedication and effort. Approach each setback as a stepping stone.

Reflection Question: How do you talk to yourself after facing a setback? Are you encouraging or critical? Practice saying, "I'm improving with each attempt," and notice the shift in your mindset.

Mental Strategies for Boosting Confidence Before Test Day

Confidence doesn't just come from knowing the material; it's built from believing in your ability to perform well on test day. Preparing your mind is as crucial as preparing your knowledge. Here are mental strategies to help boost your confidence as you approach the SAT.

1. **Visualization Technique**
   Picture yourself on test day. Imagine yourself walking into the testing center calm and prepared. Visualize each section, tackling each question with focus and clarity. Research shows that visualization can significantly reduce anxiety and improve performance.

Exercise: Close your eyes and take a few deep breaths. Picture yourself succeeding on the SAT. Imagine feeling confident and composed. Practice this daily leading up to the test.

2. **Positive Affirmations**

   The way you talk to yourself matters. Repeating positive affirmations can build confidence and reduce self-doubt. Simple statements like, "I am capable and prepared" or "I will do my best" can have a powerful impact on your mindset.

Challenge for You: Write down three affirmations that make you feel empowered. Place them somewhere visible and repeat them each day, especially in moments of doubt.

3. **Mindfulness and Breathing Exercises**

   Test anxiety can creep in, but managing it is key to maintaining confidence. Practicing mindfulness can help you stay grounded and calm. Take a few deep breaths when you feel tense, allowing your mind to return to the present moment.

Mindfulness Practice: Set aside five minutes daily to focus on your breathing. Inhale deeply, hold, and exhale slowly. This exercise helps calm the nervous system and can be used during moments of stress on test day.

Interactive Section: Challenge for You

Create a **Setback Action Plan**. Next time you face a setback—whether it's a low practice score or a challenging study day—refer to this plan. Write down three specific actions you can take to bounce back. For instance:

- **Re-evaluate my study strategy for this week.**

- **Speak to a mentor or tutor about my challenges.**

- **Practice positive self-talk.**

Keeping an action plan on hand can help you stay focused and resilient, reminding you that setbacks are part of the journey.

Key Takeaways:

- **View setbacks as stepping stones**, not failures.

- **Build resilience** by focusing on growth and maintaining a positive inner dialogue.

- **Boost confidence with mental strategies** like visualization, affirmations, and mindfulness.

Success Story: Sofia's Road to Confidence

Sofia's initial practice scores were far from her target. She struggled, especially with math, and found herself doubting her abilities. But with each setback, she learned to reframe her thinking. She began using visualization and affirmations, telling herself, "I am ready for this." With time, she improved her scores and felt confident walking into the test room on the day of the SAT.

Your SAT journey may have its ups and downs, but remember: resilience is built one challenge at a time. Each setback prepares you, strengthening your confidence and resolve. Keep pushing forward—you're on the path to success, and every step, no matter how small, brings you closer to achieving your SAT goals.

7.3 Creating a Balanced Study-Life Routine

Balancing study time with rest and personal life isn't just ideal—it's essential for long-term success. This section explores practical ways to build a sustainable routine, with downtime and relaxation woven into the study schedule. When you build a balanced approach, you avoid burnout and ensure that you're mentally and physically prepared for the SAT. Let's dive into strategies for creating this balance.

Incorporating Downtime and Relaxation into Your Study Plan

Studying hard is important, but so is knowing when to take a break. Including intentional downtime helps recharge your mind, allowing you to return to studying with fresh energy and focus. Imagine downtime as an essential part of your SAT journey—a time to pause, rejuvenate, and prepare for the next phase of work.

Example: Marco's Study Routine

Marco studied for the SAT every weekday, dedicating three hours a day after school. He noticed, however, that by Thursday, his energy dropped, and he struggled to retain information. So, Marco built in short breaks throughout his study sessions and made Friday night a time for relaxation. By reserving time for rest, he returned to studying over the weekend with more energy and focus. This helped him maintain a steady study rhythm without feeling overwhelmed.

Steps for Incorporating Downtime:

1. **Schedule short breaks** (5-10 minutes) every hour during study sessions to clear your mind.

2. **Create a designated relaxation period** each day. For instance, give yourself a full hour of rest after each intense study block.

3. **Reserve one day of the week for non-study activities** to fully recharge.

Challenge for You: Try setting a timer for your study sessions, taking five-minute breaks every 45 minutes. At the end of each session, notice how these small breaks improve your focus and retention.

How to Avoid Burnout with Effective Time Management

Burnout can sneak up when we push ourselves too hard for too long. Time management is your ally in creating a pace that's sustainable and productive. A well-planned routine keeps you on track without feeling overwhelmed, ensuring that each study session builds up to success without exhausting you.

Consider **Elena's Strategy for Avoiding Burnout**. She set up a daily study schedule with specific goals for each session—some focused on math, others on reading or writing. By rotating subjects, she prevented fatigue from overloading on one area. In addition, Elena took weekends off from studying and used that time to recharge with family activities and hobbies.

Strategies for Time Management:

1. **Prioritize tasks** by identifying the most challenging sections first, then balancing those with lighter tasks to maintain momentum.

2. **Break study time into focused blocks**, such as 45-minute sessions with designated breaks.

3. **Set clear goals for each session**, so you know exactly what you aim to accomplish each day.

4. **Rotate subjects and tasks** to prevent mental fatigue and keep things interesting.

Reflection Question: Are you pushing yourself too hard without taking breaks? What can you adjust in your routine this week to add more balance?

Maintaining Healthy Habits: Sleep, Nutrition, and Exercise

When studying for the SAT, maintaining a healthy body and mind is as important as the hours you put in. Good habits like sleeping well, eating nutritious foods, and exercising keep your brain functioning at its best, increasing concentration, memory, and resilience.

Example of Daily Routine for Balanced Health:

- **Morning**: Start with a 15-minute walk or light exercise to activate your brain.

- **Study Blocks**: Plan three to four 45-minute study sessions spaced out during the day, with breaks in between.

- **Meals**: Prioritize balanced meals with protein, healthy fats, and complex carbs to fuel your brain and body.

- **Sleep**: Aim for at least 7-8 hours each night, especially before big study days or practice tests.

Challenge for You: This week, focus on going to bed at a consistent time to establish a regular sleep schedule. After a few days, see if you notice an improvement in focus and mood.

Interactive Section: Challenge for You

Create your **Personal Study-Life Balance Plan** for this week. Write down:

- **Study sessions** for each day, with planned breaks.

- **Downtime activities** that you enjoy (movies, sports, reading for fun).

- **Physical exercise** (even just a walk or stretch) each day.

- **Bedtime goals** to ensure you're getting enough sleep.

Reflection Question: Which habits are most important for you to feel balanced and energized? Make these a priority in your weekly plan.

Key Takeaways:

- **Downtime is essential.** Regular breaks and relaxation periods help sustain your energy and motivation.

- **Effective time management** reduces burnout, keeping you focused and resilient.

- **Healthy habits** like sleep, nutrition, and exercise support peak mental and physical performance.

Success Story: Ethan's Journey to a Balanced Routine

Ethan found it hard to balance SAT prep with school and personal time. He felt stressed, and his energy was dropping fast. But after creating a more balanced routine, he saw a big difference. Ethan studied for two hours each weekday and took weekends off to spend time with friends and pursue hobbies. His sleep improved, he felt energized, and his practice test scores steadily rose. By setting a sustainable routine, he was able to prepare effectively and enjoy the process.

A balanced approach to SAT preparation is key to your success. By including rest, managing your time wisely, and building healthy habits, you're not just preparing for a test—you're setting yourself up for sustainable success. Remember, your well-being is just as important as your scores. Stay balanced, and enjoy the journey to your SAT goals.

7.4 Overcoming Procrastination and Staying on Track

Procrastination is the silent enemy of progress. It's tempting to put off studying when distractions arise, but developing the ability to stay focused and consistent is key to reaching your SAT goals. This section provides techniques to tackle procrastination, set up accountability systems, and build daily and weekly habits that will keep you on track. Let's dive into strategies that will help you conquer procrastination, stay motivated, and build a routine that supports consistent progress.

Techniques to Combat Procrastination and Stay Focused

Procrastination often starts with small distractions—a quick check of social media, a sudden interest in tidying your room, or simply telling yourself, "I'll start studying in just a minute." But when these moments add up, valuable study time slips away. Here are some effective techniques to help you take control and stay focused.

1. **The Five-Minute Rule**
    One way to tackle procrastination is with the "five-minute rule." Tell yourself you'll study for just five minutes. Often, the hardest part is simply getting started, and this technique helps reduce that initial resistance. Once you're in motion, it's much easier to continue.

2. **Set Clear, Achievable Goals for Each Session**
    Instead of vague goals like "study math," try setting specific goals like "complete five practice questions on algebra." This gives you a clear endpoint, making the task feel more manageable.

3. **Use a Distraction-Free Study Environment**
    Choose a quiet space, turn off your phone or place it in another room, and remove other potential distractions. Set up your study area with only the materials you need to keep your focus sharp.

4. **Practice the Pomodoro Technique**
    This time-management method involves studying in short, focused intervals (usually 25 minutes) with a five-minute break in between. After completing four intervals, take a longer break. This technique breaks your study session into manageable parts, making it easier to maintain focus.

Challenge for You: Try the five-minute rule today. Pick a study topic, set a timer for five minutes, and commit to starting. At the end of those five minutes, decide if you want to continue. Notice how simply starting can shift your mindset.

Using Accountability Systems to Stay Committed to Your Study Plan

Accountability can be a powerful motivator. When you share your goals with others, it creates a sense of commitment that helps you stick to your plan. Let's explore ways to make accountability work for you.

Example: Alex and His Accountability Partner

Alex struggled with consistency in his study schedule. To combat this, he teamed up with a friend who was also preparing for the SAT. They checked in with each other weekly to review their progress, celebrate successes, and discuss any challenges. Knowing someone was keeping him accountable helped Alex stay on track.

Ways to Build Accountability:

1. **Find an Accountability Partner**
   Connect with a friend, family member, or classmate who is also preparing for the SAT. Schedule regular check-ins, share your weekly goals, and hold each other accountable.

2. **Join a Study Group**
   Study groups provide structure and motivation. Even meeting once a week with peers can keep you engaged and provide encouragement.

3. **Use Accountability Apps**
   Apps like Habitica, Focusmate, or even simple to-do list apps allow you to track your progress, set reminders, and share your goals with friends for added motivation.

4. **Announce Your Goals Publicly**
   Sometimes, telling someone about your goals—even on social media or in a family chat—can make you feel more committed to achieving them.

Reflection Question: Who could you reach out to as an accountability partner? How might sharing your goals with someone help you stay on track?

Tools for Creating Daily and Weekly Study Habits

Establishing daily and weekly study habits is essential for keeping up the momentum. Consistency over time beats bursts of last-minute cramming, helping you build knowledge gradually and without added stress. Here are tools to help you create study habits that fit into your routine.

1. **Daily Study Planner**
   Use a planner or digital tool to outline your daily study tasks. Write down exactly what you'll be studying each day—this reduces indecision and keeps you focused on specific goals.

2. **Weekly Review Sessions**
   Schedule one day each week to review what you've studied. Reflect on your progress, identify areas that need more attention, and adjust your plan accordingly. Weekly reviews prevent you from forgetting previous topics and give you a clear sense of improvement.

3. **Habit-Tracking Apps**
   Apps like Streaks or HabitBull can track your study habits and visualize your progress over time. Watching your "streak" of consistent study days can be highly motivating.

4. **Visual Reminders**
   Keep a study calendar where you can mark off each day that you've completed your study goals. Watching your progress build visually can be a powerful motivator, pushing you to maintain the streak.

Example: Sofia's Weekly Study Habit

Sofia created a habit of studying for 30 minutes each weekday before school. She marked her progress on a calendar, taking a moment each day to appreciate her streak. Knowing she was building this consistent habit boosted her motivation and kept her from procrastinating.

Interactive Section: Challenge for You

Create a **Weekly Study Habit Tracker**. List your study goals for each day, such as "Tuesday: 30 minutes of SAT Reading practice," and mark off each goal you complete. At the end of the week, review your progress, note any challenges, and plan for the next week. Try to keep a streak going—each week you complete can motivate you to continue.

Reflection Question: What small daily habit could you add this week to move closer to your SAT goals? Consider setting aside a specific time each day for SAT prep, even if it's just 15 minutes to start.

Key Takeaways:

- **Overcome procrastination** by starting small, using focused study methods, and removing distractions.

- **Leverage accountability** through partners, groups, or apps to stay committed to your study plan.

- **Build daily and weekly habits** that support steady progress and keep you on track.

Success Story: James's Journey to Beating Procrastination

James struggled with procrastination, often delaying SAT study sessions. He decided to try the Pomodoro Technique, setting specific goals for each 25-minute session. He also teamed up with a friend as an accountability partner. Together, they set small goals each week, and checking in regularly kept him motivated. Gradually, James's focus improved, and he no longer felt the urge to put off his studies. By sticking to his routine, he entered test day feeling prepared and confident.

Procrastination may feel powerful, but with the right tools and strategies, you can take control of your time and stay on track. By establishing a study routine, embracing accountability, and creating habits that support your progress, you're setting yourself up for success. Every small step you take builds resilience, leading you closer to achieving your SAT goals with confidence and clarity.

7.5 Visualizing Your Success: The Power of Positive Thinking

Visualization and positive thinking are powerful tools for building confidence and mental resilience as you prepare for the SAT. Imagine yourself succeeding, completing each question with focus and ease, and seeing your target score. Visualization helps your brain believe in your success, boosting both motivation and performance. In this section, you'll explore practical techniques for visualization, discover the benefits of positive thinking, and be inspired by stories from students who turned mental strength into SAT success.

How to Use Visualization Techniques to Stay Motivated

Visualization is like a mental rehearsal. By picturing your success in detail, you prime your brain to recognize what's possible, making the real thing feel achievable and less intimidating. Here's how to practice visualization effectively.

1. **Create a Clear Picture of Test Day Success**
   Find a quiet space, close your eyes, and visualize every detail of test day: entering the testing room, taking a deep breath, and approaching each question with confidence. Picture yourself calm and focused, tackling each section with ease.

2. **Include All the Senses**
   What does success look, sound, and feel like? Imagine the satisfying sound of the timer as you complete each section, the feel of the pencil as you jot down answers, and the sense of accomplishment as you finish strong. Engaging all the senses makes visualization more powerful.

3. **Practice Daily**
   Dedicate a few minutes each day to your visualization exercise. This consistent practice reinforces confidence, helping you approach the SAT with a winning mindset.

Example: Anna's Visualization Practice
Anna was nervous about test day. She decided to try visualization, picturing herself calm and in control as she went through each section. Over time, her fears lessened, and when test day came, she felt a sense of familiarity and ease. The visualization practice made her feel as though she had already succeeded, helping her achieve a higher score than she expected.

Challenge for You: Take five minutes each day this week to visualize your SAT success. Focus on one section of the test each day, picturing yourself completing it confidently and effectively. Notice how this practice affects your mindset over time.

The Role of Positive Thinking in Improving Test Performance

Positive thinking doesn't mean ignoring challenges; it means focusing on possibilities rather than limits. Cultivating a positive mindset can transform the way you approach both studying and test day. Positive thinking is a tool that builds resilience and opens you up to better performance by shifting your focus to what's within your control.

Strategies for Building Positive Thinking:

1. **Replace Negative Thoughts with Positive Ones**
   Catch yourself when negative thoughts arise, such as "I'm not good at math." Replace it with a constructive statement like "I'm improving my math skills with each practice session." This shift makes your brain focus on progress instead of obstacles.

2. **Celebrate Small Wins**
   Each time you complete a study session or improve in a particular area, take a moment to acknowledge your success. Positive reinforcement helps maintain motivation and builds a sense of accomplishment.

3. **Set Daily Affirmations**
   Positive affirmations, like "I am prepared and capable," can help reframe your outlook. Write down a few affirmations and repeat them daily, especially on days when motivation feels low.

Example: Luke's Positive Mindset Transformation
Luke often doubted his abilities, especially in reading comprehension. He began replacing negative thoughts with affirmations like "I can improve with practice" and celebrated small improvements. This shift in perspective transformed his approach, and he gradually saw his scores rise. Positive thinking helped Luke build confidence, proving to himself that he could succeed.

Reflection Question: What are some of the negative thoughts you might have about the SAT? How can you reframe these into positive, empowering statements?

Success Stories from Other High-Scoring SAT Students

Hearing about others' successes can be incredibly motivating, especially when you see that they started in a similar place. Here are stories from students who used positive thinking and visualization to achieve impressive SAT scores.

Sophia's Journey to a 1500

Sophia aimed high, but she started with a score of 1200 on her first practice test. She struggled with test anxiety and often felt overwhelmed. Instead of giving up, she began visualizing her success daily, imagining herself confident and focused during each section. She also practiced positive thinking, repeating affirmations like, "I can and will improve." With time, her practice scores rose steadily, and on test day, she scored a 1500. Visualization and positivity became the foundation of her success.

Ethan's Transformation Through Visualization

Ethan faced difficulties in math and often doubted his abilities. He set a goal of 1400 and used visualization techniques to stay motivated. Every night before bed, he would close his eyes and imagine himself finishing the SAT math section with confidence. Over time, this practice helped calm his nerves and boosted his confidence. On test day, Ethan scored even higher than his target, crediting his daily visualization for helping him stay calm and focused.

Interactive Section: Challenge for You

Create your **Personal Visualization Routine** for the next week:

1. **Set a time each day** (morning, before studying, or before bed).

2. **Choose one section to visualize** (math, reading, or writing).

3. **Picture yourself succeeding**—approaching each question confidently, managing your time well, and feeling a sense of accomplishment.

Keep a journal to reflect on how visualization impacts your confidence and motivation. Over time, you'll see how this mental practice can support real-life success.

Key Takeaways:

- **Visualize success daily** to build familiarity and confidence for test day.

- **Use positive thinking** to reinforce resilience and focus on what's possible.

- **Learn from others' successes** as motivation that your goals are achievable.

Success Story: Maya's Path to Belief and Success

Maya initially lacked confidence in her ability to reach her target score. She often felt discouraged, comparing herself to others. But she committed to visualization and daily affirmations, repeating "I am capable, and I will succeed." Gradually, her scores improved, and so did her confidence. On the day of the test, Maya walked in with self-assurance, scoring higher than she had ever imagined. Visualization and positivity helped her realize her potential.

Visualization and positive thinking are essential tools on your SAT journey. By picturing yourself succeeding, you're training your mind for success, building confidence that will carry you through test day. With each day you practice, you're one step closer to reaching your SAT goals. Stay focused, stay positive, and remember—your belief in yourself is one of the most powerful assets you have.

Conclusion: Your Path to Digital SAT Success

As you reach the end of this guide, take a moment to appreciate all the strategies, tips, and exercises you've tackled in preparation for the Digital SAT. Your journey has covered every angle, from understanding the unique structure of the digital test to developing personalized approaches for each section. Through customized study plans, mastery of digital tools, and targeted math, reading, and writing practices, you've built a strong foundation to achieve your SAT goals.

Key Strategies Recap

In this book, you learned to:

- **Create a personalized study plan** based on your strengths and areas for improvement, ensuring every study session is efficient and focused.

- **Adapt to the digital test format,** from using the on-screen calculator effectively to practicing with digital simulators to build familiarity with test-day tools.

- **Master each section** with targeted strategies: time-saving techniques in Math, active reading skills in Reading, and precision-driven approaches in Writing.

- **Stay resilient** with mindset and motivational tips to keep you engaged and on track, even when the path seemed challenging.

Stay Motivated and Aim High

Remember, preparing for the SAT is as much a mental challenge as it is an academic one. Setbacks, whether in practice scores or challenging topics, are stepping stones, not roadblocks. Keep your goals in sight, celebrate each milestone, and embrace every small improvement. Confidence grows with practice and persistence, so trust in the work you've put in and know that you're fully capable of achieving your target score.

Next Steps

As you complete your SAT prep journey, here are some final steps to keep your momentum going:

1. **Schedule a final full-length practice test** in a timed setting, focusing on areas that still need improvement. Use this to fine-tune any last-minute strategies.

2. **Review your personalized study plan** to ensure you're as prepared as possible for the test day.

3. **Plan your test-day routine,** including relaxation techniques to help you approach the test with a calm, focused mind.

With all the tools and strategies you've gained, you're ready to conquer the Digital SAT. Now, go confidently toward your goal, knowing you have the knowledge, skills, and determination to succeed. Your hard work has set the stage—now it's time to shine. Good luck!

Digital SAT Practice Test

Section 1: Math (No Calculator)

Multiple Choice Questions

1. If 5x - 7 = 18, what is the value of x?

   o A) 3

   o B) 5

   o C) 7

   o D) 9

2. Which of the following expressions is equivalent to 3(x + 4) - 2x?

   o A) x + 4x + 4x + 4

   o B) x + 12x + 12x + 12

   o C) 3x + 43x + 43x + 4

   o D) 5x + 12

3. What is the solution to the equation 2y + 6 = 18?

   o A) 3

   o B) 6

   o C) 9

   o D) 12

4. The sum of three consecutive integers is 33. What is the smallest of these integers?

   o A) 9

   o B) 10

   o C) 11

   o D) 12

5. If a = 3 and b = -2, what is the value of 2a + 3b?

- A) 0
- B) 1
- C) 2
- D) 5

6. What is the value of 32 - 4 × 2?

- A) 1
- B) 3
- C) 5
- D) 7

7. If x - 5 = 12, what is the value of 3x?

- A) 17
- B) 21
- C) 36
- D) 51

8. Simplify: 5(x + 2) - 3x.

- A) 2x + 2
- B) 2x + 10
- C) 5x + 2
- D) 5x + 10

9. What is the value of x that makes the equation $x^2 - 4x = 0$ true?

- A) 0
- B) 2
- C) 4
- D) Both A and B

10. A rectangle has a length of 3x and a width of x. If the area of the rectangle is 48, what is the value of x?

- A) 2
- B) 4
- C) 6
- D) 8

11. If $f(x) = x^2 - 3x + 4$, what is the value of $f(2)$?

- A) 2
- B) 4
- C) 6
- D) 8

12. Solve for y: $4y - 7 = 3y + 9$.

- A) 2
- B) 3
- C) 7
- D) 16

13. If $2x + 5 = 15$, what is the value of $x + 2$?

- A) 3
- B) 5
- C) 7
- D) 9

14. The average of x, x + 2, and x + 4 is 10. What is the value of x?

- A) 6
- B) 8
- C) 10
- D) 12

15. In a triangle, the three angles are represented by x, x + 10, and 2x - 20. If the sum of the angles is 180 degrees, what is the value of x?

- A) 50

- B) 60

- C) 70

- D) 80

16. Which of the following is a solution to the equation $x^2 - 5x + 6 = 0$?

- A) 1

- B) 2

- C) 3

- D) 4

17. The expression $x^2 - 16$ is equivalent to:

- A) $(x - 4)(x + 4)$

- B) $(x - 8)(x + 2)$

- C) $(x - 2)(x + 8)$

- D) $(x - 4)^2$

18. If the equation $3(x - 2) = 2x + 5$ holds, what is the value of x?

- A) -1

- B) 1

- C) 3

- D) 5

19. What is the slope of the line that passes through the points $(1, 2)$ and $(3, 6)$?

- A) 2

- B) 3

- C) 4

- D) 5

20. Which of the following is equivalent to $(2x + 3)(x - 4)$?

- A) $2x^2 - 8x + 3$

- B) $2x^2 - 5x - 12$

- C) $2x^2 - x - 12$

- D) $2x^2 - 11x - 12$

Grid-In Questions

21. If $4x - 5 = 15$, what is the value of x?

22. A number is divided by 3, and then 4 is added to the result. If the final result is 10, what was the original number?

23. The product of two consecutive even integers is 48. What is the smaller integer?

24. If $y = 3x + 2$ and $y = 17$, what is the value of x?

25. A rectangle has an area of 60 square units and a length of 12 units. What is the width of the rectangle?

Answer Key: Section 1: Math (No Calculator)

1. B) 5	14. B) 8
2. D) $5x + 12$	15. B) 60
3. B) 6	16. B) 2
4. B) 10	17. D) $(x - 4)^2$
5. A) 0	18. C) 3
6. A) 1	19. B) 3
7. C) 36	20. A) $2x^2 - 8x + 3$
8. B) $2x + 10$	21. $x = 5$
9. D) Both A and B	22. The original number is 18.
10. B) 4	23. The smaller integer is 6.
11. B) 4	24. $x = 5$

12. B) 3	25. The width is 5 units.
13. B) 5	

Section 2: Math (With Calculator)

Multiple Choice Questions 1-15

1. If x=3 and y=4, what is the value of $2x^2 + 3y$?

   o   A) 24

   o   B) 30

   o   C) 34

   o   D) 36

2. The function $f(x)=2x^2 - 5x + 3$. What is the value of f(4)?

   o   A) 11

   o   B) 15

   o   C) 19

   o   D) 23

3. What is the average of the following set of numbers: 12, 15, 18, 20, 25?

   o   A) 17

   o   B) 18

   o   C) 20

   o   D) 21

4. If the equation $y = 3x + 2$ is graphed on a coordinate plane, what is the slope of the line?

   o   A) -3

- B) -2
- C) 2
- D) 3

5. In a survey of 150 students, 90 said they preferred studying in the morning. What percentage of the students prefer studying in the morning?

    - A) 30%
    - B) 40%
    - C) 50%
    - D) 60%

6. What is the solution to 3x - 5 = 2x + 4?

    - A) -9
    - B) -5
    - C) 5
    - D) 9

7. If $g(x)=x^2 - 4x + 7$, what is the value of $g(2)$?

    - A) -1
    - B) 1
    - C) 3
    - D) 7

8. In a school, 20% of the students are in the chess club. If there are 300 students in total, how many students are in the chess club?

    - A) 20
    - B) 40
    - C) 60
    - D) 80

9. The median of the set {3, 7, 8, 10, 12} is:

    ○ A) 7

    ○ B) 8

    ○ C) 9

    ○ D) 10

10. Which of the following equations has a slope of -2 and passes through the point (1, 3)?

    ○ A) $y = -2x + 5$

    ○ B) $y = -2x + 7$

    ○ C) $y = 2x - 3$

    ○ D) $y = -x + 3$

11. If the function $h(x) = 4x + 1$ represents the total cost of buying x items, what is the total cost of buying 5 items?

    ○ A) 15

    ○ B) 16

    ○ C) 20

    ○ D) 21

12. What is the range of the function $f(x) = x^2 - 4$ when $-2 \leq x \leq 2$?

    ○ A) $-4 \leq f(x) \leq 4$

    ○ B) $-4 \leq f(x) \leq 0$

    ○ C) $-2 \leq f(x) \leq 2$

    ○ D) $0 \leq f(x) \leq 4$

13. If 12% of a number is 36, what is the number?

    ○ A) 300

    ○ B) 360

    ○ C) 400

    ○ D) 450

14. If the probability of choosing a red marble from a jar is 1/4, what is the probability of **NOT** choosing a red marble?

   ○ A) 1/4

   ○ B) 1/3

   ○ C) 1/2

   ○ D) 3/4

15. If $3x - y = 10$ and $x = 4$, what is the value of y?

   ○ A) 2

   ○ B) 3

   ○ C) 5

   ○ D) 7

Open-Ended Questions 16-25

16. The average (arithmetic mean) of 4, 8, and x is 10. What is the value of x?

17. If $4x + 5 = 21$, what is the value of x?

18. A rectangle has a length of 10 and an area of 60. What is the width of the rectangle?

19. If $f(x) = 3x - 7$ and $f(x) = 8$, what is the value of x?

20. If 5% of a number is 25, what is the number?

21. The sum of three consecutive integers is 33. What is the smallest of the three integers?

22. If $6a + 3 = 27$, what is the value of a?

23. If a car travels at a speed of 60 miles per hour for 2.5 hours, how many miles does it travel?

24. The mean of a set of numbers is 8. If the sum of the numbers is 64, how many numbers are in the set?

25. If $x^2 - 4x = 12$ and $x > 0$, what is the value of x?

Answer Key: Section 2: Math (With Calculator)

1. B) 30	14. D) 3/4
2. D) 23	15. D) 7
3. B) 18	16. 18
4. D) 3	17. 4
5. D) 60%	18. 6
6. D) 9	19. 5
7. C) 3	20. 500
8. C) 60	21. 10
9. B) 8	22. 4
10. A) $y = -2x + 5$	23. 150
11. D) 21	24. 8
12. A) $-4 \leq f(x) \leq 4$	25. 6
13. A) 300	

Section 3: Reading

Instructions: Read each passage and answer the questions that follow. Choose the best answer for each question.

Passage 1: Literature

Passage Excerpt
This passage is adapted from Charlotte Brontë's "Jane Eyre" (1847), a novel about the journey of a young woman as she faces numerous challenges and self-discoveries.

"It is in vain to say human beings ought to be satisfied with tranquility: they must have action; and they will make it if they cannot find it. Millions are condemned to a stiller doom than mine, and millions are in silent revolt against their lot. Nobody knows how many rebellions, besides political rebellions, ferment in the masses of life which people earth."

Questions

1. **What is the primary tone of the passage?**

   o A) Resigned

   o B) Defiant

   o C) Humorous

   o D) Apologetic

2. **Which of the following best describes the author's view of human nature in the passage?**

   o A) Humans are content with tranquility.

   o B) Humans need action and struggle.

   o C) Humans are peaceful by nature.

   o D) Humans often avoid difficult situations.

3. **The word "ferment" in the last sentence most nearly means:**

   o A) grow rapidly.

   o B) dissolve.

   o C) weaken.

   o D) remain hidden.

4. **The phrase "still doom" in line 2 suggests that the author believes some people are:**

   o A) content with life.

   o B) quietly suffering.

   o C) destined for greatness.

   o D) ignorant of struggle.

Passage 2: Historical Analysis

Passage Excerpt

This passage discusses the early days of the American Revolution and the ideological shift that led to the colonies' pursuit of independence.

"By the 1770s, many American colonists had grown weary of British rule, frustrated by taxes imposed without representation and restrictions on their freedoms. Pamphlets circulated throughout the colonies, urging citizens to consider the prospect of independence. What once seemed unthinkable—a complete break from Britain—soon became a vision worth fighting for. Figures like Thomas Paine and his pamphlet 'Common Sense' helped to fuel this shift, offering a powerful argument that America had the right and duty to establish its own government."

Questions

5. **The primary purpose of the passage is to:**

    o   A) describe the British response to the American Revolution.

    o   B) explain why the American colonists decided to pursue independence.

    o   C) highlight the peaceful negotiation for independence.

    o   D) discuss Thomas Paine's biography.

6. **The phrase "vision worth fighting for" suggests that:**

    o   A) independence was a challenging yet necessary goal.

    o   B) the colonists were uncertain about independence.

    o   C) America was well-prepared for independence.

    o   D) Britain supported the idea of American independence.

7. **What role did Thomas Paine's pamphlet "Common Sense" play according to the passage?**

    o   A) It advocated for improved British rule.

    o   B) It ignited the colonists' belief in independence.

    o   C) It discouraged colonists from revolting.

    o   D) It introduced new laws to the colonies.

8. **The author's attitude toward the American pursuit of independence can best be described as:**

    o A) neutral.

    o B) disapproving.

    o C) supportive.

    o D) indifferent.

Passage 3: Science

Passage Excerpt

This passage discusses recent advancements in renewable energy and the potential of solar power.

"With global temperatures rising, scientists and engineers have been driven to innovate in the field of renewable energy. Solar power, one of the most abundant sources of clean energy, has gained significant traction. New developments in solar technology have made it possible to harness more energy from sunlight than ever before. While some argue that the initial costs of solar installation remain a barrier, advocates point to its long-term economic and environmental benefits. In a world grappling with the consequences of climate change, solar energy represents a promising step toward a sustainable future."

Questions

9. **The primary purpose of the passage is to:**

    o A) discuss the drawbacks of solar energy.

    o B) highlight the advancements and benefits of solar power.

    o C) explain how solar power works.

    o D) suggest that renewable energy is unnecessary.

10. **According to the passage, one potential obstacle to solar energy adoption is:**

• A) environmental impact.

• B) initial cost of installation.

• C) availability of sunlight.

- D) lack of public interest.

11. **The phrase "grappling with the consequences of climate change" suggests that:**

- A) the world has mostly overcome climate change.

- B) climate change is a distant concern.

- C) climate change is currently affecting society.

- D) scientists are ignoring climate change.

12. **The tone of the passage is best described as:**

- A) pessimistic.

- B) skeptical.

- C) optimistic.

- D) indifferent.

Passage 4: Social Analysis

Passage Excerpt

This passage examines the effects of modern technology on interpersonal relationships and communication.

"With the rise of digital communication, individuals now connect across vast distances in seconds. While this has brought people closer together, it has also raised questions about the depth of these connections. Studies suggest that increased screen time correlates with a decline in face-to-face interaction, possibly affecting emotional closeness. Some experts argue that digital communication, though convenient, lacks the nuances of in-person conversation, such as body language and tone, which can lead to misunderstandings."

Questions

13. **The primary concern raised by the author is that:**

- A) technology is too complicated.

- B) digital communication might affect the quality of human connections.

- C) people are using too many devices.

- D) technology has no benefits.

14. **The phrase "lacks the nuances of in-person conversation" suggests that digital communication:**

- A) enhances the depth of conversations.

- B) fails to capture non-verbal cues.

- C) is better for complex discussions.

- D) eliminates the need for emotions.

15. **The tone of the passage is best described as:**

- A) nostalgic.

- B) critical.

- C) humorous.

- D) celebratory.

16. **The author implies that the effect of digital communication on relationships is:**

- A) entirely negative.

- B) mostly positive.

- C) both positive and negative.

- D) indifferent.

Answer Key: Section 3 - Reading

Passage 1: Literature

1. **Answer:** B) Defiant

2. **Answer:** B) Humans need action and struggle.

3. **Answer:** A) grow rapidly.

4. **Answer:** B) quietly suffering.

Passage 2: Historical Analysis

5. **Answer:** B) explain why the American colonists decided to pursue independence.

6. **Answer:** A) independence was a challenging yet necessary goal.

7. **Answer:** B) It ignited the colonists' belief in independence.

8. **Answer:** C) supportive.

Passage 3: Science

9. **Answer:** B) highlight the advancements and benefits of solar power.

10. **Answer:** B) initial cost of installation.

11. **Answer:** C) climate change is currently affecting society.

12. **Answer:** C) optimistic.

Passage 4: Social Analysis

13. **Answer:** B) digital communication might affect the quality of human connections.

14. **Answer:** B) fails to capture non-verbal cues.

15. **Answer:** B) critical.

16. **Answer:** C) both positive and negative.

Section 4: Writing and Language

Instructions: Read each sentence or passage and choose the best answer to correct or improve it.

Questions 1-15: Grammar and Syntax

1. **Each of the students in the classroom have their own project to work on.**

   o A) have its own project to work on

   o B) have their own project to work on

   o C) has its own project to work on

   o D) has their own project to work on

2. **The chef, along with his assistants, are preparing the meal for tonight's event.**

   o A) are preparing the meal for tonight's event

   o B) were preparing the meal for tonight's event

   o C) is preparing the meal for tonight's event

   o D) prepares the meal for tonight's event

3. **The team of scientists were excited to present their findings at the conference.**

   o A) were excited to present their findings at the conference

   o B) was excited to present their findings at the conference

   o C) are excited to present their findings at the conference

   o D) is excited to presenting their findings at the conference

4. **Neither the manager nor the employees was aware of the changes in policy.**

   o A) was aware of the changes in policy

   o B) were aware of the changes in policy

   o C) is aware of the changes in policy

   o D) are aware of the changes in policy

5. **If anyone calls for me, tell them that I will be back shortly.**

   o A) tell them that I will be back shortly

- o B) tell him or her that I will be back shortly

- o C) tell it that I will be back shortly

- o D) tell him that I will be back shortly

6. **The research findings, though controversial, is crucial for understanding the issue.**

    - o A) is crucial for understanding the issue

    - o B) are crucial for understanding the issue

    - o C) was crucial for understanding the issue

    - o D) were crucial for understanding the issue

7. **The audience was thrilled by the performance, they gave a standing ovation.**

    - o A) by the performance, they gave a standing ovation

    - o B) by the performance; they gave a standing ovation

    - o C) by the performance and they gave a standing ovation

    - o D) by the performance because they gave a standing ovation

8. **She, not her brother, deserve the credit for the project's success.**

    - o A) deserve the credit for the project's success

    - o B) deserves the credit for the project's success

    - o C) deserve the credit because of the project's success

    - o D) deserves credit for the project's success

9. **The committee discuss the proposal every month to review progress.**

    - o A) discuss the proposal every month to review progress

    - o B) discussed the proposal every month to review progress

    - o C) discusses the proposal every month to review progress

    - o D) has discussed the proposal every month to review progress

10. **Her attitude towards the project, and her enthusiasm were infectious.**

   o   A) towards the project, and her enthusiasm were

   o   B) towards the project; her enthusiasm were

   o   C) towards the project and her enthusiasm was

   o   D) towards the project, and her enthusiasm was

11. **Each one of the students need to bring their own supplies.**

   o   A) need to bring their own supplies

   o   B) needs to bring their own supplies

   o   C) need to bring his or her own supplies

   o   D) needs to bring his or her own supplies

12. **The photographer, as well as the journalists, were scheduled to arrive at noon.**

   o   A) were scheduled to arrive at noon

   o   B) are scheduled to arrive at noon

   o   C) is scheduled to arrive at noon

   o   D) have been scheduled to arrive at noon

13. **The principal and the teachers believes that the event will be a success.**

   o   A) believes that the event will be a success

   o   B) believes that the event could be a success

   o   C) believe that the event will be a success

   o   D) believe that the event is going to be a success

14. **There is many reasons why students enjoy this teacher's class.**

   o   A) is many reasons why students enjoy this teacher's class

   o   B) are many reasons why students enjoy this teacher's class

   o   C) is one reason why students enjoy this teacher's class o   D) are many reasons why students enjoys this teacher's class

15. **Each of the following items were donated by local businesses.**

   o   A) were donated by local businesses

   o   B) was donated by local businesses

   o   C) were donated from local businesses

   o   D) has donated by local businesses

Questions 16-30: Sentence Improvement

16. **The scientist attempted to carefully analyze the data before making any conclusions.**

   o   A) to carefully analyze the data

   o   B) to analyze carefully the data

   o   C) to analyze the data carefully

   o   D) to analyze the carefully data

17. **To prepare for the trip, Maria packed her clothes, maps, and that she made sure to bring her phone charger.**

   o   A) that she made sure to bring her phone charger

   o   B) made sure to bring her phone charger

   o   C) her phone charger was packed

   o   D) brought her phone charger

18. **The professor reviewed the lecture notes thoroughly, in addition to providing detailed feedback.**

   o   A) thoroughly, in addition to providing detailed feedback

   o   B) thoroughly and provided detailed feedback

   o   C) thoroughly; also provided detailed feedback

   o   D) thoroughly provided detailed feedback

19. **The project not only requires a significant amount of time, but also needing careful planning.**

   o A) but also needing careful planning

   o B) but also careful planning

   o C) but also needs careful planning

   o D) but also needed careful planning

20. **After the play, the actor's interview was both informative, it was entertaining.**

   o A) both informative, it was entertaining

   o B) both informative, and it was entertaining

   o C) both informative and entertaining

   o D) informative as well as entertaining

Answer Key: Section 4 - Writing and Language

1.	D	11.	D
2.	C	12.	C
3.	B	13.	C
4.	B	14.	B
5.	B	15.	B
6.	B	16.	C
7.	B	17.	B
8.	B	18.	B
9.	C	19.	C
10.	D	20.	C

Bonuses

Access the bonuses, click on the link or scan the qr-code

Link: bit.ly/3YtyMFg

Made in United States
Troutdale, OR
12/28/2024

27347948R00130